W9-BKT-832

A special thank you to our stitched together story contributors for this issue of BLOCK. We love our customers and the stories you share with us are priceless. We are ever grateful for the gift of being a small part of the lives you touch.

STITCHED TOGETHER STORY CONTRIBUTORS
Jean Miller, Linda Schnakenberg, Mitzie Lepka, Alisa Simpson, Michelle Heber, Holli Besse, Keith Wycoff

EXECUTIVE EDITORS
Mike Mifsud, Alan Doan, Jenny Doan, Sarah Galbraith, David Mifsud

MANAGING EDITOR
Natalie Earnheart

CREATIVE DIRECTOR
Christine Ricks

PHOTOGRAPHY TEAM
Mike Brunner, Lauren Dorton, Jennifer Dowling, Dustin Weant

PATTERN TEAM
Edie McGinnis, Denise Lane, Jessica Woods, Gregg Allnutt

PROJECT DESIGN TEAM
Jenny Doan, Natalie Earnheart, Janet Yamamoto

EDITOR & COPYWRITERS
Jenny Doan, Natalie Earnheart, Christine Ricks, Katie Mifsud, Camille Maddox, Nichole Spravzoff, Edie McGinnis

SEWIST TEAM
Jenny Doan, Natalie Earnheart, Janet Yamamoto, Carol Henderson, Denise Lane, Janice Richardson, Jamey Stone

QUILTING & BINDING DEPARTMENT
Sarah Richardson, Betty Bates, Karla Zinkand, Natalie Loucks, Debbie Elder, Jan Meek, Angela Wilson, Chelsea White, Mary McPhee, Charlene McCabe, Dennis Voss, Debbie Allen, Jamee Gilgour, Michelle Templeton, Frank Jones, Kara Snow, Ethan Lucas, Devin Ragle, Bruce VanIperen, Lyndia Lovell, Aaron Crawford, Cyera Cottrill, Deborah Warner, Salena Smiley, Francesca Flemming, Rachael Joyce, Bernice Kelly, Deloris Burnett

PRINTING COORDINATORS
Rob Stoebener, Seann Dwyer

PRINTING SERVICES
Walsworth Print Group
803 South Missouri
Marceline, MO 64658

CONTACT US
Missouri Star Quilt Company
114 N Davis
Hamilton, Mo. 64644
888-571-1122
info@missouriquiltco.com

content

Oops! Sometimes we make mistakes.
To find corrections to every issue of Block
go to: **www.msqc.co/corrections**

hello
from MSQC

Summertime is upon us with plenty of pool parties, backyard barbecues, and roadtrips to be had. My guess is the last thing that's on your mind is the upcoming holiday season, but this month we wanted to give you the gift of time. That's why we've planned a holiday issue filled with wonderful ideas for handmade gifts you can actually make with time to spare! If I've learned anything from the age-old story of the grasshopper and the ant, it's that I could always use more time for ideas, thinking, and planning. I tend to be more like that carefree grasshopper, singing its heart out in the summer sun, and when the winter comes, I dislike feeling rushed and unprepared. So it's time I've learned my lesson and started early for once!

The first thing to do is start by making a simple list. Don't overwhelm yourself, just jot down who you *need* to make things for and who you *want* to make things for. Those are two different lists. In our family we draw names for holiday gift-giving and then I know who I need to make something for. Then I add people to my list that I want to make things for. I prioritize by finishing the needs first and then I start on the wants. Also, if making a big quilt causes you to break out in hives just thinking of it, make a few blocks instead and create a table runner, a potholder, a pillow, or a tote bag. All are beautiful, useful gifts.

Once you've got a plan in place, you can check off things one by one throughout the summer and fall, and when winter comes, you'll be able to sit back and enjoy the holidays more fully. So, all my dear friends, this issue is for you. It'll help all of us get a handle on the holidays before they are upon us. After all, time passes so quickly. Enjoy the moment while you can because before you know it, it will be a memory.

JENNY DOAN
MISSOURI STAR QUILT CO

TRY OUR APP

It's easy to keep up on every issue of BLOCK magazine. Access it from all your devices. And when you subscribe to BLOCK, it's free with your subscription! For the app search BLOCK magazine in the app store. Available for both Apple and Android.

MISSOURI STAR
QUILT CO.

PPEARING PINWHEEL
SHOOFLY

quilt pattern for 10" squares

75¾" x 87"

handmade
just for you

Have you ever received a handmade gift? I hope the answer is yes! It's one of my favorite kinds of gifts because I'm a maker myself and I appreciate the time and effort that goes into creating a handmade gift. But even more than receiving, I enjoy making and giving handmade gifts. I get so excited when I get an idea for a gift that I know the receiver will absolutely love. In the process of making it I think about how it will be used and enjoyed. I believe that all the love and excitement I experience goes into the object I'm creating. It fills my heart with love, and in return fills someone else's heart with love as well.

The holiday season is very special to me. More than the gifts and parties, I appreciate the renewed focus on others. And the great thing is, as makers we get to feel that all year round! When we make something and give it away, each time we have a renewal of that love and kindness returned to us again and again. My hope for each of you is that every project you create will be filled with love and that love will return to you tenfold. Merry making!

CHRISTINE RICKS
MSQC Creative Director, BLOCK MAGAZINE

PRINTS

FBY54568 Shiny Objects - Holiday Twinkle Spot On Snow Metallic by Flaurie and Finch for RJR Fabrics
SKU: 3164-004

FBY55816 Howdy - Horseshoes Pink Yardage by Stacy Iset Hsu for Moda Fabrics
SKU: 20555 19

FBY56415 Llama Navidad - Llama Navidad Aqua by Michael Miller Fabrics for Michael Miller
SKU: CX7383-AQUA-D

FBY54282 Holly Jolly Christmas - Candy Cane Stripe Ivory by Mary Lake Thompson for Robert Kaufman
SKU: AMK-16652-15

FBY54937 Merry Scriptmas - Greetings Evergreen by Moda Fabrics for Moda Fabrics
SKU: 33263 15

FBY55069 A Time of Wonder - Snowflakes Green by Gina Linn for Blank Quilting
SKU: 8609-66

SOLIDS

FBY1168 Bella Solids - White Bleached by Moda Fabrics for Moda Fabrics
SKU: 9900 98

FBY1695 Bella Solids - Betty's Pink from Moda Fabrics
SKU: 9900 120

FBY12148 Bella Solids - Breeze by Moda Fabrics
SKU: 9900 132

FBY1696 Bella Solids - Betty's Red from Moda Fabrics
SKU: 9900 123

FBY57824 Bella Solids - Basil by Moda Fabrics for Moda Fabrics
SKU: 9900 330

FBY1284 Bella Solids Christmas Green by Moda Fabrics
SKU: 9900 14

*For the tutorial and everything
you need to make this quilt visit:*
www.msqc.co/blockholiday17

9-patch on point

During the holiday season, our thoughts often turn toward giving as we wrap up presents for our loved ones. I've heard so many inspiring stories about quilters caring for others and I often get asked how Missouri Star gives back to our community. Here's one way we do our part to help.

Each year we host a Christmas Giveback to benefit our friends and neighbors. I read recently that in the United States alone, one in five children are hungry. It's hard to imagine that there are little ones who go without when we have so much on our own plates. So last December we decided to focus on the local elementary school and supplied food boxes for their Backpack Buddies program.

Over the weekends, when children don't have access to school meals, some go hungry for long stretches of time. Backpack Buddies bridges the gap between home and school, providing kids with a backpack full of food to last them until the following Monday. Nationwide, over half of our children qualify for free lunches, so this program meets a vital need. Working together, the MSQC family gathered enough food to last the children though the end of winter break, which can be a tough time for families in need.

Each department "adopted" food boxes and filled them with necessities for children to take home over the holidays. A total of forty-five boxes were filled and returned just in time for school to be out. Our kind employees went over the top with their generosity! I am so grateful to be a part of such a thoughtful group of people. When asked about the project, their responses filled my heart. They said things like, "We are part of an amazing and giving company. We can do this!" and

"I just love that we were able to back and help these kids have meals and comfort! It really brings the true meaning of Christmas to heart!" To me, that is what the Christmas spirit is all about.

This holiday season, it's important to remember that there are people in need right in our own backyards. We're already making plans for the next Christmas Giveback and I'm excited to see what we can do this year. There are so many opportunities to do good each day. Don't wait for the holidays to begin looking for ways to give. Start today and keep in mind that no matter what we do, our efforts, large and small, truly make a difference in this world.

materials

QUILT SIZE
75½" X 84"

BLOCK SIZE
8½" finished

QUILT TOP
1 roll of 2½" print strips
3½ yards background fabric

INNER BORDER
¾ yard

OUTER BORDER
1½ yards

BINDING
¾ yard

BACKING
5¼ yards - vertical seam(s)

SAMPLE QUILT
Holiday Flourish 10 by Peggy Toole
for Robert Kaufman

1 cut

From the background fabric, cut:
- (15) 2½" strips across the width of the fabric
- (16) 5¼" strips across the width of the fabric – subcut each strip into (7) 5¼" squares for a **total of 112.**

2 make strip sets

Select 18 print strips from the roll. Set aside the remainder of the strips for another project.

3 strip set a

Sew a print 2½" strip to either side of a background 2½" strip with right sides facing. Press the seam allowances toward the print strips. **Make 7** strip sets and cut each strip set into (16) 2½" increments for a **total of 112. 3A**

4 strip set b

Sew a background 2½" strip to either side of a print 2½" strip with right sides facing. Press the seam allowances toward the print strip.

3A

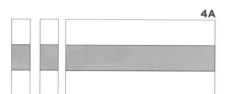

4A

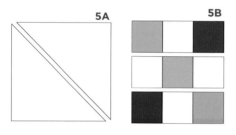

5A

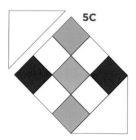

5B

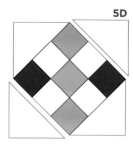

5C

5D

Make 4 strip sets and cut each strip set into 2½" increments for a **total of 56.** 4A

NOTE: *You'll have 8 pieces left over to use for another project.*

5 block construction

Cut (2) 5¼" background squares from corner to corner once on the diagonal. **5A**

Sew a 2½" increment from strip set A to either side of a 2½" increment from strip set B to complete a 9-patch block. **5B**

Sew a background triangle to 2 opposite sides of the 9-patch block. Add a background triangle to the 2 remaining sides of the 9-patch. **Make 56** blocks and square each to 9" to make an 8½" finished block. **5C, 5D**

6 arrange and sew

Lay out the **blocks in rows.** Each row is made up of 7 blocks and 8 rows are needed. After the blocks have been sewn into rows, press the seam allowances of the odd-numbered rows toward the right and the even-numbered rows toward the left to make the seams "nest."

Sew the rows together to complete the center of the quilt.

7 inner border

Cut (7) 2½" strips across the width of the fabric. Sew the strips together end-to-end to make one long strip. Trim the borders from this strip.

Refer to Borders (pg. 111) in the Construction Basics to measure and cut the inner borders. The strips are approximately 68½" for the sides and approximately 64" for the top and bottom.

8 outer border

Cut (8) 6½" strips across the width of the fabric. Sew the strips together end-to-end to make one long strip. Trim the borders from this strip.

Refer to Borders (pg. 111) in the Construction Basics to measure and cut the outer borders. The strips are approximately 72½" for the sides and approximately 76" for the top and bottom.

9 quilt and bind

Layer the quilt with batting and backing and quilt. After the quilting is complete, square up the quilt and trim away all excess batting and backing. Add binding to complete the quilt. See Construction Basics (pg. 111) for binding instructions.

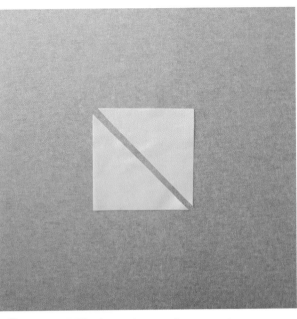

1 Sew a 2½" print strip to either side of a 2½" background strip to make strip set A. Sew a 2½" background strip to either side of a 2½" print strip to make strip set B. Cut 2½" increments from both.

2 Cut (2) 5¼" background squares from corner to corner once on the diagonal. Set aside for the moment.

3 Sew a piece from strip set A to each side of a piece from strip set B to make a 9-patch block.

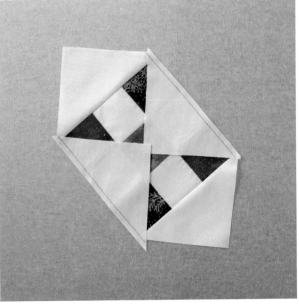

4 Stitch a background triangle to 2 opposite sides of the 9-patch block.

5 Add a background triangle to the 2 remaining sides of the 9-patch.

6 Press the block and square it to 9".

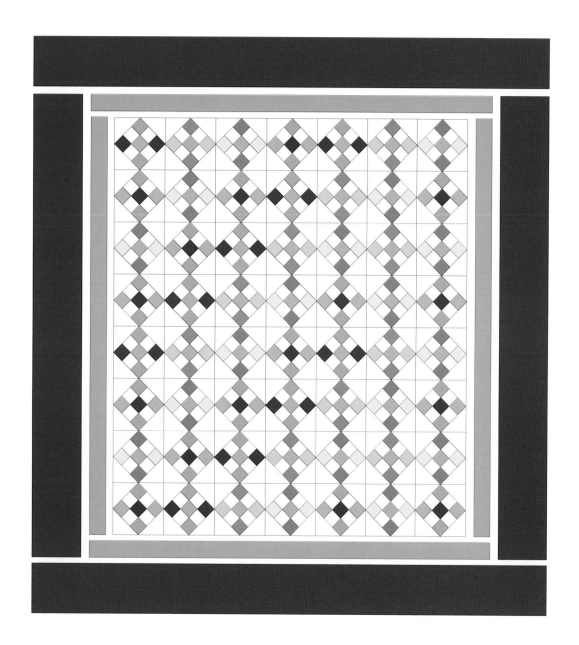

For the tutorial and everything you need to make this quilt visit:
www.msqc.co/blockholiday17

baby
blocks

story contribution by Jean Miller

Sharing Christmas with a child is a magical experience. It is so fun to watch their eyes light up with each new toy. But too much of a good thing can be overwhelming, and when the toy room is filled to overflowing, it's hard for those little ones to truly enjoy what they have.

Jean loved to spoil her little great-niece with gifts, but soon discovered that even children know the wonder of a handmade quilt.

Christmas is magical when you're a kid. Toys and toys and more toys. I decided that enough was enough and I wasn't going to continue giving toys to my great-niece, Alison, any longer so I decided she would receive a quilt on Christmas and her birthday instead.

Alison's first Christmas quilt was a Snoopy and Charlie Brown theme, and I was worried that gift would go over like a lead balloon. Much to my surprise, she opened the quilt, took one look, then wrapped herself up in it and smiled. She was only a year old, and it absolutely melted my heart.

Fast forward to Christmas 2016. I had suffered a shoulder injury and had been unable to quilt for four months. I knew there would be no quilt this year, but I figured that four-year-old Alison wouldn't notice. I bought her several little gifts and made a cute tower of presents.

The gift opening began. She started on her tower and worked her way down politely thanking me for each box. When she got to her final box, which was only about eight inches square, she turned to look at me and asked, "Is this my quilt?" My heart dropped. I explained that there wasn't one this year because my shoulder was hurt and I couldn't

sew. Her reply was "Well, I guess I have enough quilts already," but the look on her face was one of total heartbreak.

I would have never thought those quilts would mean so much to a child, but they have given her memories that will last a lifetime. In turn, I have had the pleasure of knowing how much my time and effort is appreciated. And you can bet Alison will never go without her Christmas quilt again as long as I am able!

materials

QUILT SIZE
42" x 42"

BLOCK SIZE
32" finished

QUILT TOP
4 assorted print 2½" x width of fabric
   strips or 1 roll of 2½" print strips
½ yard contrasting print
¾ yard background fabric

BORDER
¾ yard

BINDING
½ yard

BACKING
3 yards – vertical seam(s)

SAMPLE QUILT
Comfort and Joy by Dani Mogstad for
Riley Blake Designs

1 cut

From the contrasting fabric, cut:

- (4) 9" squares

From the background fabric, cut:

- (4) 9" squares

- (4) 8½" squares

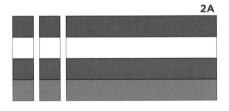

2 make a strip set

Sew (4) 2½" strips together along the

lengths. Make sure the right sides of the

strips are facing as you add each one.

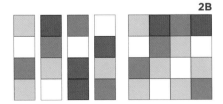

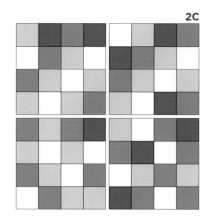

2C

Press all seam allowances in the same direction. Cut the strip set into (16) 2½" increments to make 2½" x 8½" rectangles. **2A**

Sew 4 strip-pieced rectangles together to make an 8½" square. **Make 4.** 2B

Sew the (4) 8½" squares together to make the center portion of the star. 2C

3 make half-square triangles

On the reverse side of each 9" background square, draw a line from corner to corner once on the diagonal. Layer a 9" background square with a 9" contrasting print square with right sides facing. Sew on both sides of the drawn line using a ¼" seam allowance. Cut on the drawn line, open and press the seam allowance toward the darker fabric. Each square will yield 2 half-square triangle units and a total of 8 units are needed. After each unit has been pressed, square to 8½". **3A**

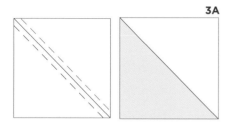

3A

4 block construction

Sew 2 half-square triangles together to make a flying geese unit. **Make 4.** 4A

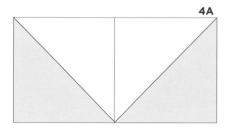

4A

To make the top and bottom row of the block, sew an 8½" background square to either side of a flying geese unit. **Make 2.** 4B

To make the center row of the block, sew a flying geese unit to either side of the center square. 4C

Sew the 3 rows together to complete the block. 4D

Block Size: 32" finished

5 border

Cut (4) 5½" strips across the width of the fabric. Sew the strips together end-to-end to make one long strip. Trim the borders from this strip.

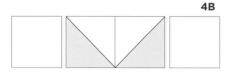

4B

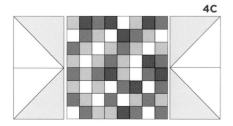

4C

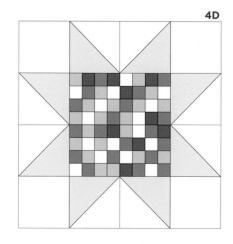

4D

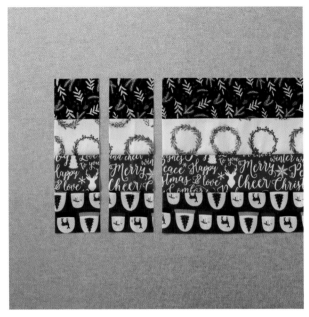

1 Sew (4) 2½″ strips together along the lengths. Cut the strip set into (16) 2½″ increments.

2 Sew 4 strip-pieced rectangles together to make an 8½″ square. Make 4.

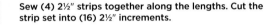

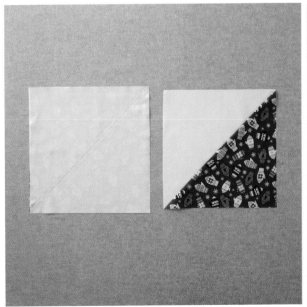

3 Draw a line from corner to corner once on the diagonal on the reverse side of a 9″ background square. Layer with a print square with right sides facing and sew on both sides of the line, using a ¼″ seam allowance. Cut on the drawn line, open each half-square triangle and press. Square to 8½″.

4 Sew 2 half-square triangles together to make a flying geese unit. Sew an 8½″ background square to either side to make the row for the top and bottom of the block. Sew the 4 strip-pieced squares together, then add a flying geese unit to either side to make the center row. Sew the rows together to complete the block.

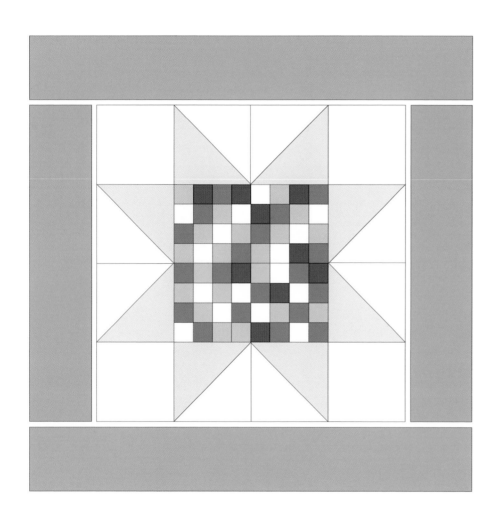

Refer to Borders (pg. 111) in the Construction Basics to measure and cut the outer borders. The strips are approximately 32½" for the sides and approximately 42½" for the top and bottom.

6 quilt and bind

Layer the quilt with batting and backing and quilt. After the quilting is complete, square up the quilt and trim away all excess batting and backing. Add binding to complete the quilt. See Construction Basics (pg. 111) for binding instructions.

candy
catcher
bag

Have you ever noticed that as you get older, teenagers start to look more and more like troublemakers?

It has always been this way. When we were teens, our grandparents were wary of our rowdy music and shaggy hair. And when our grandparents were young, they scandalized their own elders with bobbed hair and rouged knees.

To the mature observer, it seems like those rascals have too much time on their hands and too much mischief in their minds. And nothing brings out the shenanigans in a pack of teens like Halloween.

A few years ago, a sweet older lady named Hazel was facing her first winter without her dear husband, Ronald. The house was so quiet and lonely, she couldn't help but feel a bit nervous during the long, chilly nights of autumn. Every creak and bump in the night left its mark on her nerves.

As Halloween drew near, Hazel started to worry. She envisioned gangs of good-for-nothings descending on her quiet neighborhood to leave a trail of toilet paper, cracked eggs, and smashed pumpkins.

For the tutorial and everything you need to make this quilt visit:
www.msqc.co/blockholiday17

candy catcher bag

On Halloween night, Hazel handed out candy until nine o'clock. Then she turned off her front porch light, locked the door, and went straight to bed. It was just after eleven o'clock when, she was awakened by the sound of hurried footsteps just outside her window. She lay in the darkness and listened to whispering voices and stifled giggles.

Her feelings vacillated between fear and anger as she imagined the trouble that was brewing in her own front yard. Finally, she gathered her courage and ventured out to shoo those darn kids away. She threw open the front door, but she was too late. They were gone.

Hazel was about to call the police when she noticed a basket on the steps in front of her. It was filled with fragrant red apples and homegrown walnuts. Attached to the handle was a pumpkin-shaped note that read, "Happy Halloween! Love, your neighborhood goblins."

Hazel squinted her eyes and peered into the darkness, and that's when she noticed a pile of black garbage bags under her sycamore tree, filled to capacity and closed up tight. Those kids had raked up every leaf!

For Hazel, that Halloween was all treats and no tricks, and she sure was grateful for that pack of teenagers with nothing better to do than help a lonely old neighbor.

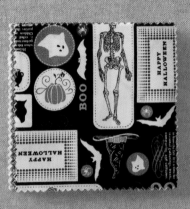

materials

BAG SIZE
13½" x 15"

SUPPLIES
1 package 5" print squares
¾ yard contrasting fabric – includes
   lining and strap
25" x 40" scrap of batting

SAMPLE BAG
Eek Boo Shriek by Carina Gardner
for Riley Blake Designs

1 outer bag

Select 21 squares from the package. Sew
(3) 5" squares together into a row. **Make
7 rows.** Sew the rows together to form a
rectangle. Set aside the remaining squares
for another project. (It's the perfect
amount to make a second bag!) **1A**

Cut a piece of batting 4" wider and longer
than the pieced rectangle. Place the
pieced rectangle on top of the batting and
quilt, using any design you like. Trim and
square up the edges.

1A

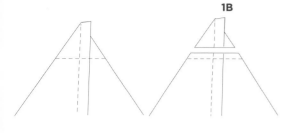

1B

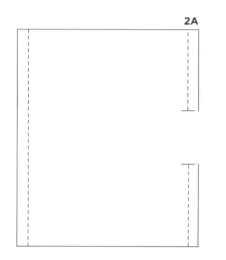

2A

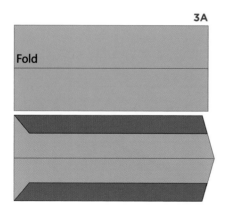

3A

Fold

Lay out the pieced rectangle on the lining fabric and cut a rectangle the same width and length.

Fold the pieced and quilted rectangle in half lengthwise with right sides facing. Sew the side seams together. After the side seams are sewn, make boxed corners by pulling on one corner of the bag until a peak is formed. Measure 1¾" from the point of the peak and draw a line straight across. Sew on the drawn line, then trim the excess fabric away ¼" from the sewn seam. Repeat for the other corner of the bag. **1B**

2 lining

Fold the lining rectangle in half lengthwise with right sides facing. Sew the side seams together leaving an opening of about 4" in one seam. Be sure to take a couple of back stitches on both sides of the opening. **2A**

Follow the directions above and make boxed corners in the lining. Set the two pieces of the bag aside for the moment while you make the strap.

3 strap

Cut (1) 1½" x 40" strip of lightweight batting.

Cut (1) 5" x 40" fabric strip. Trim the selvages off and fold the strip in half lengthwise with wrong sides together. Press. Open the strap and press both raw edges in (about ½") toward the center crease. **3A**

Open one of the folded edges and place the 1½" strip of batting between the center of the strip and the fold. Fold the strip in half along the center pressed crease and stitch the strap closed by sewing ¼" from the edge. Add two more lines of stitching by sewing ¼" in from the opposite edge and right down the center. Trim the ends of the strap to your desired length. **3B**

Turn the body of the bag inside out. Place the strap inside. Center one end of the strap to the sewn seam allowance on one side of the bag and pin in place. Repeat for the other end of the strap, and pin to the remaining seam allowance.

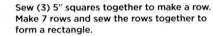

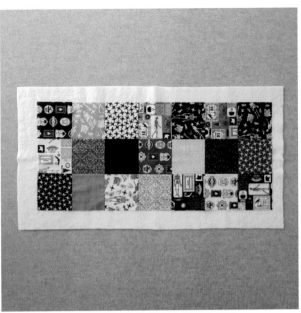

1 Sew (3) 5" squares together to make a row. Make 7 rows and sew the rows together to form a rectangle.

2 Place the pieced rectangle on top of the piece of batting and quilt as you like. Trim the excess batting away and square up the edges of the rectangle.

3 Cut a 5" x 40" fabric strip. Fold the strip in half and press with wrong sides together. Fold the raw edges in toward the center and press. Slip a 1½" x 40" strip of batting in under one fold.

4 Fold the strap in half and stitch it closed by sewing ¼" in from the edge. Add 2 more lines of stitching by sewing ¼" in from the opposite edge and right down the middle.

5 Make the lining the same size as the bag. Box the corner by pulling the corner down so it forms a peak. Measure up 1¾" from the point and draw a line straight across. Sew on the drawn line, then trim the excess fabric away ¼" from the sewn seam.

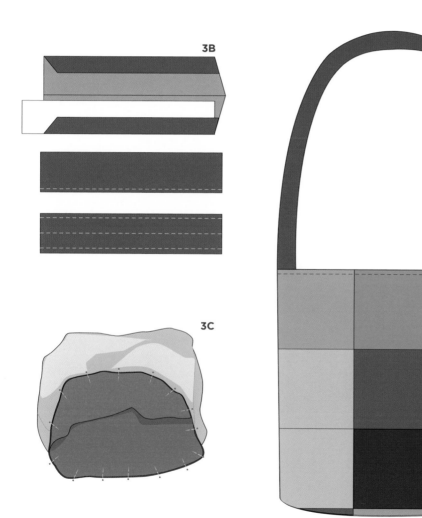

3B

3C

Turn the lining right side out. Drop it into the bag - notice that the right sides are facing each other. Align the side seam allowances and pin in place through all three layers (lining, bag, and strap). Pin the lining to the bag in several more places. Start on a side seam and sew all the way around the top using a seam allowance a bit wider than ¼". **3C**

Reach into the bag and find the opening that was left in the side seam of the lining. Pull the whole bag through the opening to turn it right side out. After turning, whipstitch the opening in the lining closed and tuck inside the bag.

Top stitch around the top about ¼" from the edge to complete the bag.

crossing
paths

story contribution by Linda Schnakenberg

Quilters love to give homemade gifts, but if you don't start your holiday projects early, that last-minute scramble can leave you with half-finished Christmas presents.

Many of us have started with big plans to make a home-made gift, then ended up with an unbound quilt or an unfinished top come Christmas. But I know of one gal who beats us all; she took twenty-five years to finish her Christmas quilt!

Linda had learned to sew at her grandmother's side. She was only thirteen years old when her mother passed away, and those sewing lessons allowed her to connect with her Grandma and hone a skill that would be useful throughout her life.

As an adult, Linda sewed curtains, pillows, and the occasional article of clothing, but she was the mother of two young sons and a full-time high school English teacher. She just didn't have much time for hobbies.

It was during this busy phase of life that Linda discovered quilting, namely a pattern called The Eight-Hour Quilt. It

For the tutorial and everything you need to make this quilt visit:
www.msqc.co/blockholiday17

crossing paths quilt

was a giant star created from 14½" right triangles and squares. The pattern took little time to create, and as easy as it was, it always turned out beautiful—even with less than perfect stitches.

Knowing that her sister would enjoy a quilt of her own, she bought fabric, cut it out, and waited for some free time to sew a Christmas quilt.

But before she had a chance to work on that quilt, her father became gravely ill. Linda spent every minute she could at the hospital until he passed away on December 17th. Between grieving, the funeral, Christmas programs at school for her children, and end-of-semester grading, Linda had no time to finish her sister's quilt. She decided to wrap the pieces with a note explaining that she would finish it and give it to her later. Ah, good intentions! Once the holidays were over, she was back to full-time teaching and taking care of her family. The quilt pieces were put away and forgotten.

Twenty-five years later, Linda retired and rediscovered her love of sewing and quilting. One day, while looking for scraps in the storage room, she pulled out a tub of 14½" right triangles and squares. She had found her sister's quilt!

Linda decided to keep the discovery a secret. She quickly finished the top and had it quilted with a beautiful design. Once it was bound, she packaged it up and drove to her sister's home. When the package was opened her sister screamed, "You found my quilt!" After twenty-five years, she had finally received her Christmas gift!

materials

QUILT SIZE
63" X 73"

BLOCK SIZE
10" finished

QUILT TOP
1 roll of 2½" print strips
1¼ yards light fabric – includes
   inner border

OUTER BORDER
1 yard

BINDING
¾ yard

BACKING
4 yards - horizontal seam(s)

SAMPLE QUILT
Forever Green by Holly Taylor for
Moda Fabrics

1 cut

From the light fabric, cut:

- (10) 2½" strips across the
  width of the fabric – set
  aside the remaining fabric
  for the inner border.

2 make strip sets

Sew a light 2½" strip to a print 2½"
strip using a ¼" seam allowance.
Add 3 more 2½" strips. You should
have 5 strips sewn together and
the light strip should be on the top.
Make 10. 2A

2A

2B

3A

Sew the top row to the bottom row with right sides facing. You now have a tube. **2B**

3 cut

Cut the tube into (15) 2½" increments across the width of the strip. Each tube set should yield enough strips for 3 blocks. Keep the strips grouped together. **3A**

3B

Pick up a 2½" strip of sewn pieces. Remove the thread in the seam allowance between row 5 and row 1. This should put the light piece at the top. **3B**

Open the next 2½" strip set in the same manner between row 1 and row 2, the next between row 2 and row 3, etc., until you have opened all 5 strips. **3C**

3C

4 sew

Sew the opened strips together to complete 1 block. **Make 30 blocks. 4A**

Block Size: 10" finished

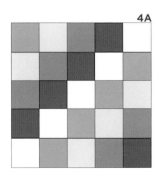

4A

5 arrange and sew

Arrange the blocks into rows. Each row has 5 blocks across. **Make 6 rows.**

Press the seam allowances of the odd-numbered rows toward the right and the even-numbered rows toward the left. Sew the rows together.

6 inner border

Cut (6) 2½" strips across the width of the fabric. Sew the strips together end-to-end to make one long strip. Trim the borders from this strip.

Refer to Borders (pg. 111) in the Construction Basics to measure and cut the inner borders. The strips are approximately 60½" for the sides and approximately 54½" for the top and bottom.

7 outer border

Cut (7) 5" strips across the width of the fabric. Sew the strips together end-to-end to make one long strip. Trim the borders from this strip.

Refer to Borders (pg. 111) in the Construction Basics to measure and cut the outer borders. The strips are approximately 64½" for the sides and approximately 63½" for the top and bottom.

8 quilt and bind

Layer the quilt with batting and backing and quilt. After the quilting is complete, square up the quilt and trim away all excess batting and backing. Add binding to complete the quilt. See Construction Basics (pg. 111) for binding instructions.

1 Sew 4 print 2½" strips together along the length. Add a light 2½" strip to the top to complete 1 strip set. Make 10.

2 Sew the top row to the bottom row with right sides facing. You now have a tube.

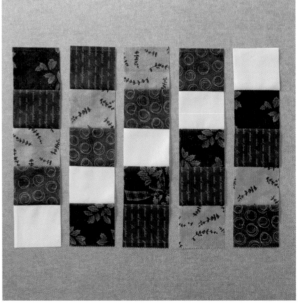

3 Cut each tube into (15) 2½" increments. Keep the strips cut from each strip set grouped together.

4 Pick up a loop of sewn pieces. Remove the thread in the seam allowance between row 5 and row 1. Open the next seam between row 1 and 2, then row 2 and row 3, etc. Once all strips have been opened, sew them together to complete the block.

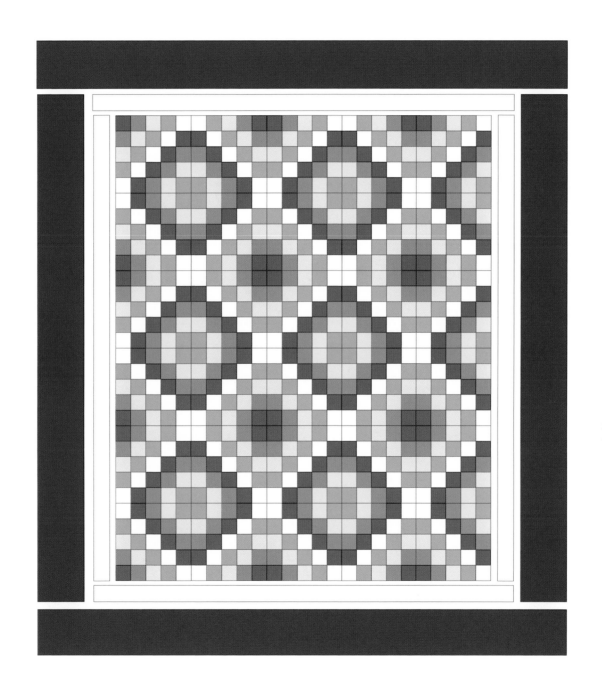

fancy fan
table topper

When I walk into our machine quilting department here at MSQC, sometimes I feel like we're like the elves at the North Pole, stitching away on all your beautiful quilts so you can give them to the people you love. Delicious home baked goods are another wonderful way of showing you care. Pair up any homemade gift with a plate of cookies and it's a winner. Liz Hawkins of Mama Hawk's Bakery here in Hamilton has a fantastic cookie recipe you'll want to squirrel away for the holidays. She also shared a story that will definitely make you smile.

One year I came home from college in December, so excited for my mom's Christmas cookies. She made the best Christmas treats that we'd eat all winter break! But this particular year I got home and there were no cookies. None! I was devastated. The thought of those cookies got me through finals! And ... nothing? My mom explained that she was on a diet so she wouldn't be making them that year. I was appalled and heartbroken at the same time. Moms should never diet in December, okay? My mom told me if I wanted them so bad, I could make them myself. And that's when I became the official family Christmas Cookie Baker.

For the tutorial and everything
you need to make this quilt visit:
www.msqc.co/blockholiday17

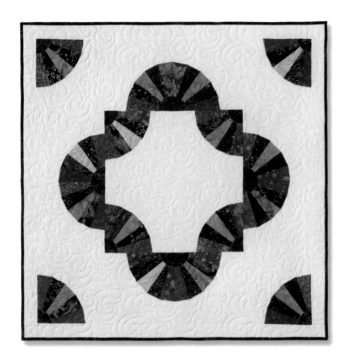

MAMA HAWKS
Christmas Sugar Cookies

1⅓ cup butter, salted
1⅓ cup granulated sugar
2 eggs
1 tsp vanilla paste

½ tsp salt
1 T cornstarch
4½ cup flour

In a large bowl cream together butter and sugar. Add eggs and vanilla. Mix until combined. Add salt, cornstarch and flour until fully incorporated. Roll out on parchment paper and refrigerate for 1 hour. Remove from refrigerator and cut out shapes from cold dough. Bake at 350° for 7 minutes. Decorate as desired and eat!

From that time on, I've continued baking and it's become an important part of my life. In my mind, it's all about creativity. It's like fabric. You're taking the same basic ingredients and creating something new and different. It's not that different from quilting, painting, or any other type of creative outlet! It's just a different medium, although the gratification is usually a bit more instant—in the smile of a child who gets to lick the beater, or someone's face when they get a warm chocolate chip cookie straight from the oven. It's like serving up happiness every single day.

Sharing love in this way is a family tradition during the holiday season. We give plates or tins of cookies to friends and neighbors. I spend the entire month of December baking and preparing. I make family favorites from when I was a kid: fudge, chocolates, toffee bars, chocolate peppermint cookies, and sometimes mini loaves of cranberry banana orange bread. On Christmas Eve, we package the cookies, along with cards, and deliver them. Sometimes we carol and sometimes we leave packages on porches and doorbell ditch!

I believe that baking communicates a deep sense of caring. I have found that home-baked treats are a rare thing these days. People don't have time. We've become so accustomed to commercial baked goods with preservatives and weird ingredients no one can pronounce. So when you get a box of freshly baked yummy goodness, with real butter, sugar, and lots of love baked in there, well, I think people experience what I call "the Grinch effect." You know, where your heart grows three sizes and you're suddenly bursting with the Christmas spirit!

materials

TABLE TOPPER SIZE
42" X 42"

BLOCK SIZE
9½" finished

TABLE TOPPER
1 package 5" print squares
¼ yard complimentary print fabric
1½ yards background fabric -
  includes border

BINDING
½ yard

BACKING
2¾ yards - vertical seam(s)

ADDITIONAL SUPPLIES
MSQC Dresden Plate Template

SAMPLE TABLE TOPPER
Very Merry by Kathy Engle for
Island Batik

1 cut

From the complimentary fabric, cut:

*   (1) 5" strip across the width of
    the fabric. Subcut (4) 5"
    squares from the strip. Use the
    template on page 47 and cut a
    circle from each of the
    (4) 5" complimentary squares.
    Fold each circle in half twice,
    once vertically, once
    horizontally. Cut along the fold
    lines to make quarter circles. Set
    aside for the moment. **1A**

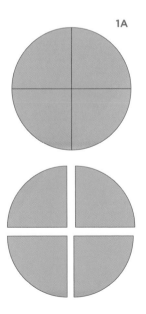

1A

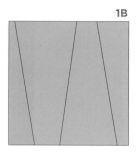

1B

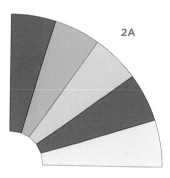

2A

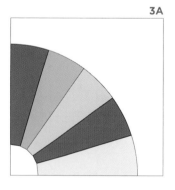

3A

From the 5" print squares, cut:

- 80 fan blades. Align the 5" mark on the template with the top of a 5" square. Cut 1 blade then flip the template 180 degrees and cut a second blade. Each 5" square will yield 2 blades. **1B**

From the background fabric, cut:

- (4) 10" strips across the width of the fabric - subcut each strip into (4) 10" squares for a **total of 16**. Set aside the remainder of the fabric for the border.

2 sew

Sew 5 blades together to make a fan. **Make 16. 2A**

3 appliqué

Using a small blanket stitch or zigzag, appliqué a fan to one corner of a 10" background square. Place a quarter circle on the corner, covering up the raw ends of the blades. Appliqué in place to complete the block. **Make 16. 3A**

Block Size: 9½" finished

4 lay out blocks

Follow the diagram on page 47 and lay out the blocks in rows. Notice how the blocks are oriented. Each row is made up of **4 blocks** and there are **4 rows.**

When you are satisfied with the arrangement, sew the blocks into rows. Then sew the rows together to complete the center of the quilt top.

5 border

Cut (5) 2½" strips across the width of the fabric. Sew the strips together end-to-end to make 1 long strip. Cut the borders from this strip.

Refer to Borders (pg. 111) in the Construction Basics to measure and cut the outer borders. The strips are approximately 38½" for the sides and approximately 42½" for the top and bottom.

6 quilt and bind

Layer the quilt with batting and backing and quilt. After the quilting is complete, square up the quilt and trim away all excess batting and backing. Add binding to complete the quilt. See Construction Basics (pg. 111) for binding instructions.

1 Use the template on page 47 to cut a circle. Cut the circle in half vertically and horizontally to make quarter circles.

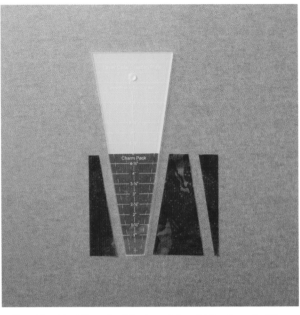

2 Align the 5" mark of the template with the top of a 5" square. Cut one fan blade, then flip the ruler 180 degrees and cut another blade.

3 Sew 5 contrasting fan blades together and appliqué to 1 corner of a 10" square.

4 Place a quarter circle on the corner, covering up the raw edges of the blades. Appliqué in place to complete the block.

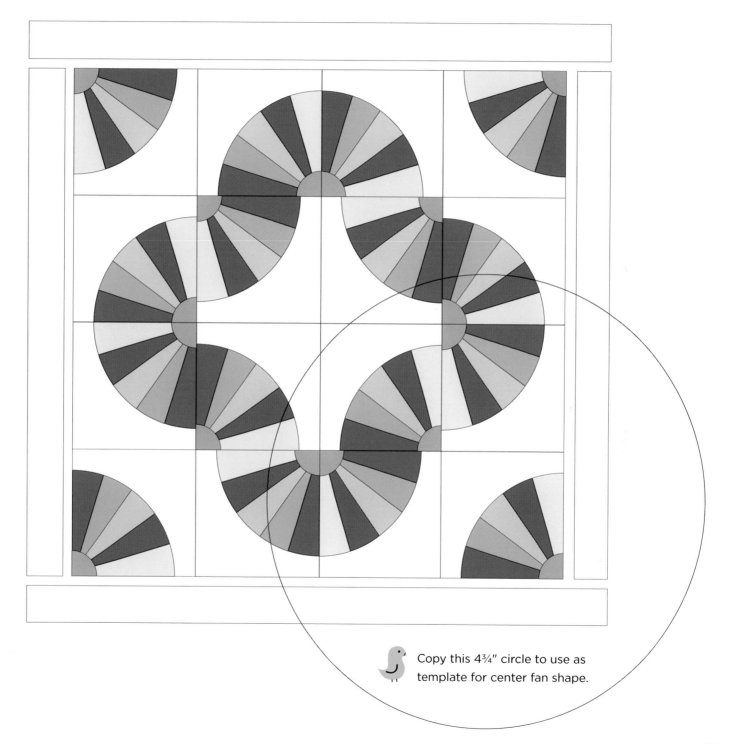

Copy this 4¾" circle to use as template for center fan shape.

garden
stars

story contribution by Keith Wycoff

The holiday season can be a difficult time for our troops serving in the armed forces. They long to be near their families, but are often far away, wishing for the warmth of home. Quilts of Valor is a wonderful organization that brings comfort through quilts. Lovingly handcrafted quilts are awarded to those who have been "touched by war" and to this day over 162,750 quilts have been given to veterans. Here at MSQC, this effort is near and dear to our hearts. We employ many veterans who have bravely served our country and we'd like to say thank you once more! This story is from Keith, a veteran who served in Desert Storm. He now works in the warehouse and happily drives a forklift.

I grew up near Hamilton, Missouri. My parents had a farm within thirty minutes of town. I joined the Navy when I was nineteen and I served for four years, from 1990 until 1994. At first I was assigned to the U.S.S. Theodore Roosevelt, one of several aircraft carriers in the Red Sea during Desert Storm. Then I went to school to become an Aviation Life Support Specialist or "Parachute Rigger" and served on the U.S.S. Seattle with my helicopter squadron. Because my job was all about safety, we had a couple of "man overboard" where people had fallen off the ship, and everything the rescuers had on was something I made. If I hadn't done my job, they

For the tutorial and everything you need to make this quilt visit:
www.msqc.co/blockholiday17

wouldn't have been able to do their jobs. I helped make almost all the equipment they used to rescue people and make sure it was operable.

After Desert Storm, I went on to become a rigger where I learned to pack and repair parachutes, and use a variety of different sewing machines. Some jokingly called me a "seamstress" and downplayed the importance of my job, but what use is a parachute with a hole in it? Initially, we had to learn how to pack our own parachutes and then later we were asked to jump with them. If I wasn't willing to jump with my own parachute, then why would anyone else want to use it? I quickly understood the importance of doing my job well.

In my helicopter squadron, I learned to make anything from flight bags to seat covers. The skills I learned repairing and making items helped me after the Navy when I worked in a car seat manufacturing plant. When seat covers were damaged, I knew how to repair them. These skills have led to many jobs and years of creating instead of buying. When something comes from your hands, nothing beats that. I'll always be grateful for the things I learned in the Navy and I just want to say thank you to those currently serving. That's really all you can say. That's what everybody said to me. Any little connection to home means so much. We're thinking about you and we love you.

Learn more about Quilts of Valor at www.qovf.org

materials

QUILT SIZE
68" X 68"

BLOCK SIZE
12" finished

QUILT TOP
1¾ yards red - includes outer border
2¼ yards background fabric -
  includes inner border
1¼ yards blue - includes corner
  stones and star points

OUTER BORDER
1¼ yards

BINDING
¾ yard

BACKING
4¼ yards – vertical seam(s)

SAMPLE QUILT
Studio Texture Delft by Timeless
Treasures
Toscana Kiss Me by Deborah
Edwards for Northcott

1 cut
From the background fabric, cut:
- (8) 5" strips across the width
  of the fabric – subcut each strip
  into (8) 5" squares for a **total of
  64 squares.**

- (8) 2½" strips across the width
  of the fabric – subcut each strip
  into (3) 2½" x 12½" rectangles
  for a **total of 24.** Set aside for
  sashing rectangles.

Set the remainder of the background
fabric aside for the inner border.

From the blue fabric, cut:
- (4) 5" strips across the width of
  the fabric - subcut each strip into
  (8) 5" squares for a **total of 32.**
- (2) 4½" strips across the width of
  the fabric - subcut each strip into
  (8) 4½" squares for a **total of 16.**

- (4) 2½" strips across the width
  of the fabric - subcut each strip
  into (16) 2½" squares for a **total
  of 64.**

There will be 7 squares left over for
another project.

From the red fabric, cut:
- (4) 5" strips across the width of
  the fabric - subcut each strip
  into (8) 5" squares for a **total
  of 32.** Set the remainder of the
  fabric aside for the outer border.

2 half-square triangles
Mark a line from corner to corner once
on the diagonal on the reverse side of
32 background squares. Layer a 5" blue
square with a marked 5" background
square with right sides facing. Sew
¼" on both sides of the drawn line.

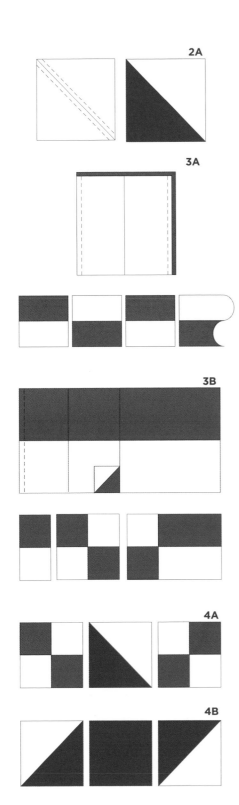

2A

3A

3B

4A

4B

Cut on the drawn line. Open to reveal 2 half-square triangles. Press the seam allowance toward the darker fabric. **Make 64** and square each to 4½". **2A**

3 4-patches

Pair a red 5" square with a background 5" square with right sides facing. Sew 2 side seams together. Cut in half, open and press the seam allowance toward the darker fabric. Sew the units together into a long strip making sure a background piece always touches a red. **3A**

Fold over the first block of the strip at the seam line and cut at 2½". You will have (1) 2-patch unit and (1) 4-patch unit. Continue to fold and cut down the length of the strip. All cuts will yield a 4-patch unit except for the very first and last cuts. Those 2-patch units can be sewn into a 4-patch. **Make 64** 4-patches. **3B**

4 block construction

Select 4 half-square triangles, (4) 4-patch units and (1) 4½" square. Sew a 4-patch to either side of a half-square triangle. **Make 2 rows. 4A**

Sew a half-square triangle to either side of the 4½" square to make the center row of the block. **4B**

Sew the 3 rows together to complete the block. **Make 16. 4C**

Block Size: 12" finished

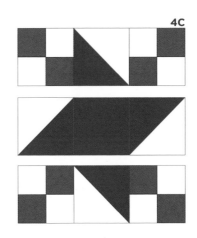

4C

5 sashing

Mark a line from corner to corner once on the diagonal on the reverse side of (48) 2½" squares cut from the blue fabric. There should be 9 squares left to use as cornerstones.

Place a marked square on each end of a 2½" x 12½" background rectangle. Sew on the marked line. Trim the excess fabric ¼" away from the sewn seam. **Make 24. 5A**

Make a long horizontal sashing strip by sewing a sashing rectangle to a 2½" square. Add another sashing rectangle, a square, and continue in this manner until you have sewn a row made up of 4 sashing rectangles and 3 squares. **Make 3. 5B**

5A

5B

1 Layer a marked 5″ background square with a 5″ blue square. Sew on both sides of the marked line using a ¼″ seam allowance. Cut on the line and open to reveal 2 half-square triangle units. Square each to 4½″.

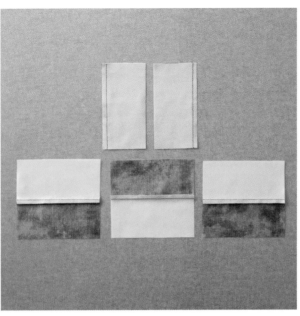

2 Pair a red 5″ square with a background 5″ square. With right sides facing, sew the 2 side seams together. Cut the sewn squares in half vertically. Open and press the seams toward the red fabric.

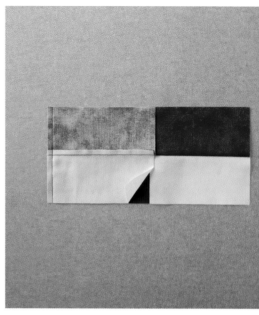

3 Sew the red and white units together into a long strip while making sure a background piece always touches a red piece.

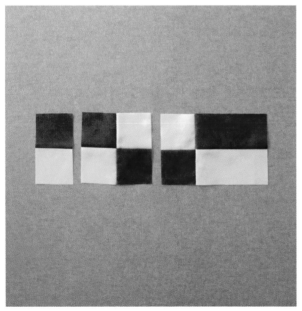

4 Fold over the first block of the strip at the seam line and cut at 2½″. Include the seam allowance in the measurement. You will have (1) 2-patch and (1) 4-patch with the first cut. Continue to fold and cut to make (64) 4-patches.

5 Sew a 4-patch unit to opposite sides of a half-square triangle unit to make the top and bottom row of the block. Sew a half-square triangle unit to opposite sides of a 4½″ square to make the center row. Sew the three rows together to complete the block.

6 lay out and sew

Lay out the blocks in rows with each row having 4 blocks across. Place a vertical sashing rectangle between each block. When you are happy with the arrangement, sew the blocks and sashing together. **Make 4 rows.** Refer to the diagram on the next column if necessary.

After the rows have been made, sew them together, adding a horizontal sashing strip between each row.

7 inner border

Cut (6) 2½" strips across the width of the fabric. Sew the strips together end-to-end to make one long strip. Trim the borders from this strip.

Refer to Borders (pg. 111) in the Construction Basics to measure and cut the inner borders. The strips are approximately 54½" for the sides and approximately 58½" for the top and bottom.

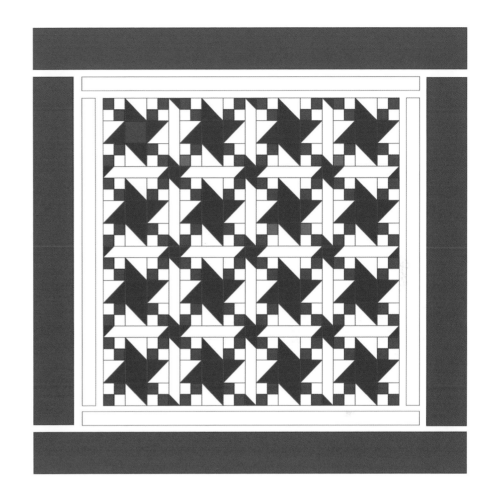

8 outer border

Cut (7) 5½" strips across the width of the fabric. Sew the strips together end-to-end to make one long strip. Trim the borders from this strip.

Refer to Borders (pg. 111) in the Construction Basics to measure and cut the outer borders. The strips are approximately 58½" for the sides and approximately 68½" for the top and bottom.

9 quilt and bind

Layer the quilt with batting and backing and quilt. After the quilting is complete, square up the quilt and trim away all excess batting and backing. Add binding to complete the quilt. See Construction Basics (pg. 111) for binding instructions.

home for christmas pillows

story contribution by Mitzie Lepka

I love to give gifts, but I sometimes struggle to come up with presents that are meaningful and wanted. I don't want to add to clutter, and I'm not always sure what sorts of gifts will be truly useful.

One fun solution to tricky gift-giving situations is to surprise your loved ones with experiences instead of "things." A weekend away from home. Tickets to a sporting event. Music lessons. An annual pass to the zoo. These types of gifts can be enjoyed together, and they create wonderful memories to last a lifetime. My personal favorite? The gift of quilting.

Mitzie had such a hard time deciding what to give her adult children for Christmas. She had requested wish lists from all her kids to be provided by Thanksgiving Day. One of her daughters was reluctant to ask for anything more extravagant than socks and underwear. Mitzie was not impressed. So she refused her daughter's boring, practical requests and

For the tutorial and everything you need to make this quilt visit:
www.msqc.co/blocksummer17

demanded something a little more special. After some prodding, the daughter finally admitted that what she really wanted was to be taught how to quilt.

Mitzie was so excited by the idea of quilting with her daughter. That was a gift that would be fun to give AND fun to receive! She said, "I bought all the tools she would need as a beginner quilter including an instruction book written by a member of my guild. I chose fabric to complete a wall hanging. Then I showed her how to use the rotary cutter and how to stitch a quarter-inch seam. Fifteen years later, she is an excellent quilter and doing longarm quilting for others. I am the proud mother of a talented daughter."

Here at Missouri Star Quilt Co, we know the joy of teaching others to quilt. Our entire focus is making this wonderful art accessible to as many people as possible. Male and female, young and old, we all have something inside us that pushes us to create, to make something beautiful and lasting and important.

This year, when you're scrambling to find something wonderful to give to your loved ones, don't despair! Perhaps they'd enjoy a yoga class or some fly fishing instruction. Or maybe, just maybe, they'd like to learn how to quilt.

materials

PILLOW SIZE
16" finished

SUPPLIES
8 contrasting print 10" squares

BACKING
½ yard

OTHER
Pillow Forms to fit or your choice
of filler – Fiberfill, etc.

SAMPLE PILLOWS
Woodland Winter by Michael Miller
Fabrics

1 make half-square triangles

On the reverse side of 4 light print
squares, draw a line from corner to
corner twice on the diagonal. Layer a
light print square with a contrasting
print with right sides facing. Sew on
both sides of each drawn line using a ¼"
seam allowance. Cut the sewn squares
in half vertically and horizontally, then
cut on the drawn lines. Open each half-
square triangle unit and press the seam
allowance toward the darker fabric.
Square each unit to 4½". Each set of

1A

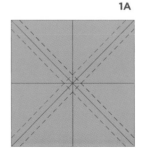

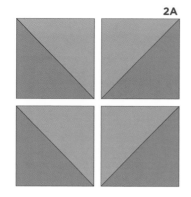

2A

sewn squares will yield 8 half-square triangle units and 16 are needed for each pillow top. 1A

2 lay out and sew

Option 1

Arrange 4 matching half-square triangles into a 4-patch quadrant as shown. **Make 2.** 2A

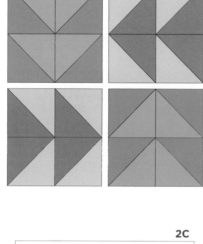

2B

Make the remaining 2 quadrants using matching contrasting half-square triangles.

Sew the 4 quadrants together to complete the pillow top. 2B

Cut a 16½" square from the backing fabric. Layer the pillow top and backing together with right sides facing. Sew the 2 pieces together by sewing all the way around the outer edge, leaving an opening on one side large enough to push the pillow form in place or for filling with stuffing. 2C

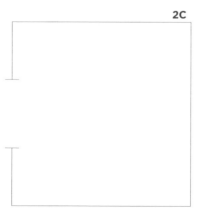

2C

Turn the pillow right side out and stuff. Whipstitch the opening closed to complete the pillow.

Option 2

Arrange 4 matching half-square triangles into a 4-patch quadrant as shown. **Make 2.** 2D

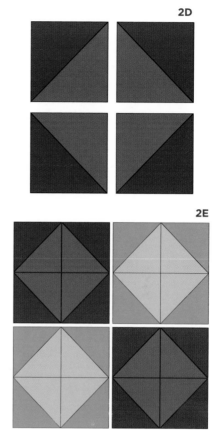

2D

2E

Make the remaining 2 quadrants using matching contrasting half-square triangles.

Sew the 4 quadrants together to complete the pillow top. 2E

Refer to the instructions under Option 1 to finish the pillow.

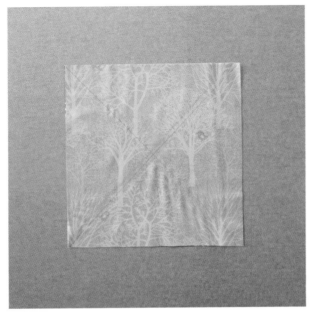

1 Draw a line from corner to corner twice on the diagonal of a light 10" square. Layer the light square with a contrasting 10" square with right sides facing. Sew ¼" on both sides of the drawn line.

2 Cut the sewn squares in half vertically and horizontally, then cut on the drawn lines. Open and press the half-square triangles open.

3 Arrange 4 half-square triangles into 2 sets of flying geese.

4 Sew the half-square triangles together as shown to make one quadrant of the block. Make 4 for each pillow.

Option 1

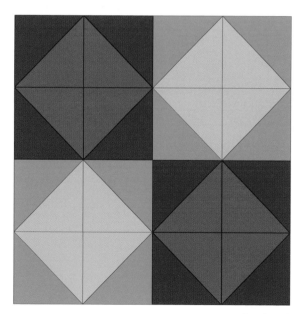

Option 2

linked
up

This was my year to be more balanced and to give more of myself. It's also been a year of growth through giving. Some time ago I attended a seminar where the speaker asked all of us to raise our hands as high as we could. Of course we all did. He paused and looked at us and said, "Now raise them a little higher," and we did. That sea of hands reminded me that it's amazing what we can do when we work together! This world may be vast, but it is made up of individuals. We are linked by the common thread of humanity. Despite our diverse experiences, our feelings are often alike.

One year ago, in June, there was a shooting at Pulse nightclub in Orlando, Florida. I believe that when tragedy strikes, there is something inside each of us that longs to reach out and help. I knew we had to do something. Right away, quilters began making heart blocks that were put together into quilts. Here at Missouri Star we joined in and invited our employees to make quilt blocks. They did a wonderful job and we sent six finished quilts to the Orlando Modern Quilt Guild so they could be distributed to those affected by the tragedy.

For the tutorial and everything you need to make this quilt visit:
www.msqc.co/blockholiday17

Just this past June I received a thank you note from the Orlando Modern Quilt Guild. Did you know they got quilts from just about everywhere? They received over 1,800 quilts! How amazing is that? When I travel I get to hear heartwarming stories like this over and over. I am so proud of what we do with the quilts that we give. This year as I spoke to groups during my trunk shows, I challenged them to make a quilt for someone

they didn't know. It's incredible what happens when we notice each other and offer support during difficult times in life.

Quilts can do so much! They can bring hope, color, warmth, comfort, and love. Wherever you are in your quilting journey, push yourself a little harder, raise your arms a little higher, and sew a few more stitches. Our world needs your love more than ever.

materials

QUILT SIZE
71" X 80½"

BLOCK SIZE
8½" finished

QUILT TOP
(1) package 5" print squares
3¼ yards background fabric –
   includes inner border
1 yard solid – sashing

BORDER
1¼ yards

BINDING
¾ yard

BACKING
5 yards - vertical seam(s)

SAMPLE QUILT
A Moose for Christmas by Cheryl
Haynes of Prairie Grove Peddler
for Benartex

1 cut

From the background fabric, cut:
- (32) 2½" strips across the width of the fabric – subcut 11 strips into 2½" x 5" rectangles. Each strip will yield 8 rectangles and you need a **total of 84.** Subcut the remaining 21 strips into 2½" x 9" rectangles. Each strip will yield 4 rectangles and you need a **total of 84.**
- (7) 1½" strips across the width of the fabric – subcut each strip into 1½" x 2½" rectangles. Each strip yields 16 rectangles and you need a **total of 97.**

From the solid sashing fabric, cut
- (10) 1½" strips across the width of the fabric – subcut each strip into 1½" x 3¾" rectangles. Each strip yields 10 rectangles and you need a **total of 98.**
- (8) 1½" strips across the width of the fabric – subcut each strip into 1½" x 8" rectangles. Each strip yields 5 rectangles and you need a **total of 40.**
- (2) 1½" strips across the width of the fabric. Subcut the strip into 1½" x 4¾" rectangles. Each strip yields 8 rectangles and you need a **total of 16.**

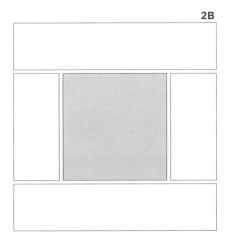

2A

2B

3A

2 sew

Sew a 2½" x 5" rectangle to either side of a 5" square. 2A

Stitch a 2½" x 9" strip to the top and bottom of the unit to complete the block. **Make 42.** 2B

Block Size: 8½" finished

3 vertical sashing rectangles

Sew a 1½" x 3¾" solid rectangle to either side of a 1½" x 2½" rectangle. **Make 49.** 3A

4 horizontal sashing strips

Begin each row with a 1½" x 2½" background rectangle, then add an 8" solid rectangle. Continue alternating the two pieces until you have sewn a strip consisting of (6) 1½" x 2½" rectangles and (5) 1½" x 8" solid rectangles. Sew a 1½" x 4¾" solid rectangle to both ends of the strip to complete 1 sashing strip. **Make 8.** 4A

4A

5 arrange and sew

Lay out the **blocks in rows** with each row having 6 blocks across. Place a vertical sashing rectangle at the beginning and end of each row and between each block. When you are happy with the arrangement, sew the blocks and sashing together. Make 7 rows. Refer to the diagram on page 71, if necessary.

After the rows have been made, sew them together, adding a horizontal sashing strip between each row. Refer to the diagram on page 71, if necessary.

Add a horizontal sashing row to the top and the bottom to complete the center of the quilt.

6 inner border

Cut (7) 2½" strips across the width of the fabric. Sew the strips together end-to-end to make one long strip. Trim the borders from this strip.

Refer to Borders (pg. 111) in the Construction Basics to measure and cut the inner borders. The strips are approximately 68" for the sides and approximately 62½" for the top and bottom.

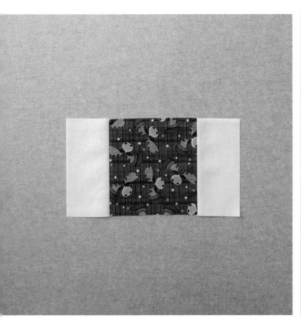

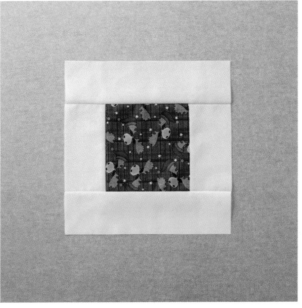

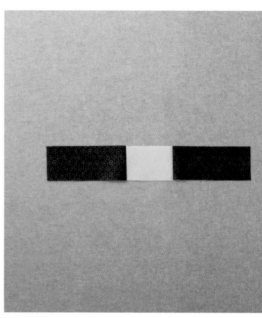

1 Sew a 2½" x 5" rectangle to either side of a 5" print square.

2 Sew a 2½" x 9" strip to the top and bottom to complete the block.

3 Sew a 1½" x 3¾" solid rectangle to either side of a 1½" x 2½" rectangle to make vertical sashing rectangles.

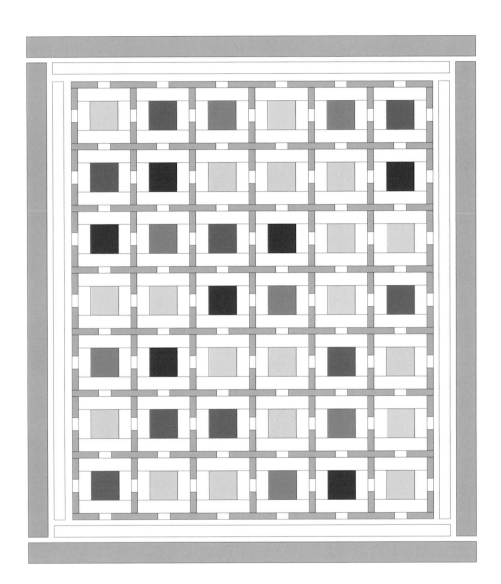

7 outer border

Cut (8) 5″ strips across the width of the fabric. Sew the strips together end-to-end to make one long strip. Trim the borders from this strip.

Refer to Borders (pg. 111) in the Construction Basics to measure and cut the outer borders. The strips are approximately 72″ for the sides and approximately 71½″ for the top and bottom.

8 quilt and bind

Layer the quilt with batting and backing and quilt. After the quilting is complete, square up the quilt and trim away all excess batting and backing. Add binding to complete the quilt. See Construction Basics (pg. 111) for binding instructions.

For the tutorial and everything
you need to make this quilt visit:
www.msqc.co/blockholiday17

ribbons
of hope

story contribution by Alisa Simpson

One in eight women will develop breast cancer over the course of her lifetime. In fact, it is estimated that over 250,000 women will be diagnosed this year alone. That's more than a quarter of a million of our dearest friends. Our mothers. Our sisters. Our daughters. Most of us have already been touched by this terrible disease in one way or another, and when those hard times come, we search for ways to help.

One group of friends held a hair-shaving party. Another organized a gigantic superhero-themed carnival to raise funds for medical bills. A ladies' church group organized babysitting and an endless stream of home cooked meals. An entire neighborhood banded together to run a landscaper's business while she underwent months of treatment.

When Alisa's mother was diagnosed with cancer, she felt helpless. So she did what many of us would do. She started to quilt.

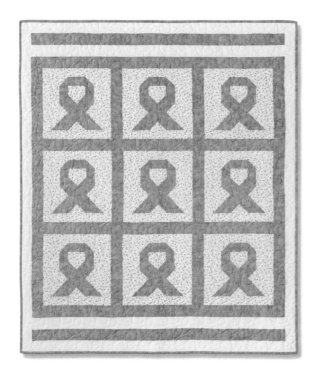

I had each of my siblings send me handprints of their kids and I embroidered them on the quilt in their favorite colors. The quilt had the name of each child and grandchild, and in the middle was emblazoned our family motto during this difficult time, "Be Strong."

This quilt was able to keep her warm and as comfortable as possible during her first round of chemo. Little did we know, the quilt's first trip to chemo would also be its only trip. My mom passed away only a few short weeks after the quilt was completed.

Before she died, my mom stated very clearly that she wanted the quilt left in her home so that when the grandchildren were visiting, they could wrap it around their shoulders and know it was a "hug from Grandma."

Her chemo quilt has become the Grandma Quilt, and was used often in those first few days after she left us. Quilting gave me the comfort of being useful and productive when there was nothing I could do to help my mom. In turn, it gave my mom a way to leave a token of her love behind with us when she passed.

There is such great power in serving others. When we give of our time and talents to show support to support a loved one, hearts are healed, even when the body is not.

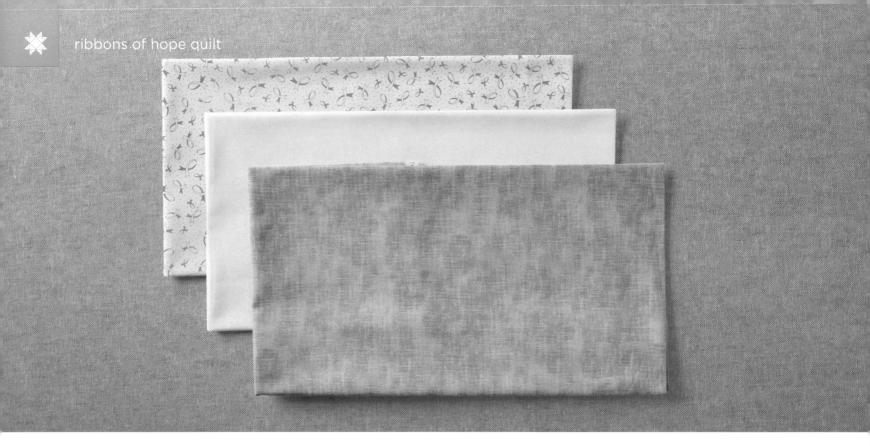

materials

QUILT SIZE
48" X 56"

BLOCK SIZE
12" finished

QUILT TOP
1½ yards pink – includes border
   strips
1½ yards background print

BORDER
¾ yard

BINDING
½ yard

BACKING
3¼ yards - horizontal seam(s)

SAMPLE QUILT
Studio Texture Pink by Timeless
Treasures

1 cut

From the pink fabric, cut:

- (5) 3½" strips across the
  width of the fabric – subcut
  4 strips into (11) 3½" squares.
  Subcut the remaining strip into
  (1) 3½" square and (9) 2" x 3½"
  rectangles.

- (1) 2" strip across the width of
  the fabric – subcut the strip into
  (18) 2" squares.

- (2) 2½" strips across the width
  of the fabric – subcut each strip
  into (3) 2½" x 12½" rectangles
  for a **total of 6.** Set aside to use
  for vertical sashing rectangles.

- (2) 2½" x 40" strips. Set aside
  for horizontal sashing strips.

Set aside the remaining fabric for
borders.

From the background print, cut:

- (1) 3½" strip across the width
  of the fabric – subcut the strip
  into (9) 3½" squares.

- (20) 2" strips across the width
  of the fabric – subcut the strips
  into the following pieces:
  - 6 strips into (3) 2" x 12½"
    rectangles for a **total of 18,**

  - 5 strips into (4) 2" x 9½"
    rectangles for a **total of 18,**

  - 4 strips into (5) 2" x 8"
    rectangles for a **total of 18,**

  - 1 strip into (9) 2" x 3½"
    rectangles,

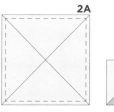

2A

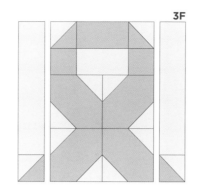

3F

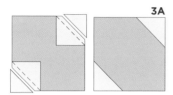

3A

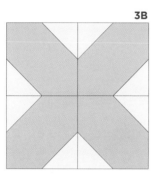

3B

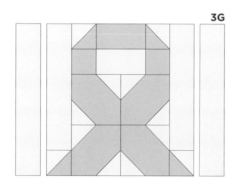

3G

3C

3D

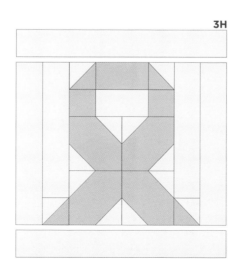

3H

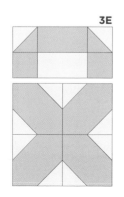

3E

• 4 strips into (20) 2″ squares for a **total of 72.** You will have 8 squares left over for another project.

2 make half-square triangles

Layer a 3½″ background print square with a 3½″ pink square with right sides facing. Sew all the way around the outer edge of the layered squares. Cut each set of sewn squares twice on the diagonal. You will have 4 half-square triangle units. Open each unit and press the seam allowance toward the darker fabric. Repeat, using the remaining 3½″ background print squares. You will have a **total of 36** half-square triangle units. Square each to 2″. **2A**

3 block construction

Mark or press a diagonal line from corner to corner once on the diagonal on each of (8) 2″ print background squares. Snowball 2 corners of a 3½″ pink square by sewing a marked square on 2 opposite sides as shown. Trim the excess fabric away ¼″ from the sewn seam. Press. **Make 4. 3A**

Sew the 4 snowballed pink squares together to make an X block. Set it aside for the moment. **3B**

Sew a 2″ pink square to both ends of a 2″ x 3½″ background print rectangle. **3C**

Sew a half-square triangle to both ends of a 2″ x 3½″ pink rectangle. **3D**

Sew the 2 rectangles together and add them to the top of the X block. **3E**

1 Layer a 3½" background print square with a 3½" pink square with right sides facing. Sew all the way round the outer edge of the squares, using a ¼" seam allowance.

2 Cut the sewn squares from corner to corner twice on the diagonal to make half-square triangle units. Square each to 2".

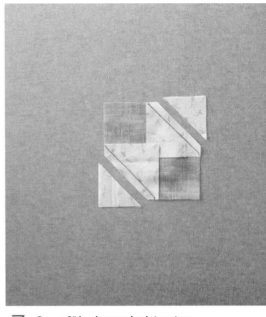

3 Sew a 2" background print on two opposite corners of a 3½" pink square with right sides facing. Trim the excess fabric away ¼" from the sewn seam.

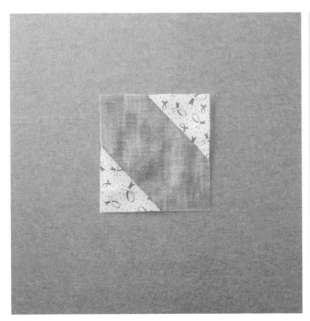

4 Open the snowballed square and press. Make 4.

5 Lay out all the pieces for the block. Sew the pieces together beginning with the center pieces and work out toward the edges.

Sew a half-square triangle to one end of a 2" x 8" background print rectangle. **Make 2** and sew one to each side of the block. **3F**

Sew a 2" x 9½" background print rectangle to either side of the block. **3G**

Add a 2" x 12½" background print rectangle to the top and bottom to complete the block.

Make 9. **3H**

Block Size: 12" finished

4 arrange and sew

Lay out the **blocks in rows**. Each row is made up of 3 blocks and 3 rows are needed. Sew a 2½" x 12½" sashing rectangle between each block as you sew each row together. After the blocks have been sewn into rows, press the seam allowances toward the sashing rectangles.

Trim the selvages from each of the 2½" x 40" horizontal sashing strips. Sew the rows together, adding a horizontal sashing strip between each row to complete the center of the quilt. Press the seam allowances of the sashing strips toward the sashing.

5 inner border

Cut (2) 2½" strips across the width of the pink fabric. Measure the quilt top from top to bottom in several places at least 6"– 8" in from the edges. Refer to Borders (pg. 111) for measuring and cutting instructions, if necessary. The quilt should measure approximately 40½". **Make 2** strips that size and sew one to either side of the quilt. Cut (5) 2½" strips across the width of the pink fabric and (3) 2½" strips across the width of the white fabric. Measure the

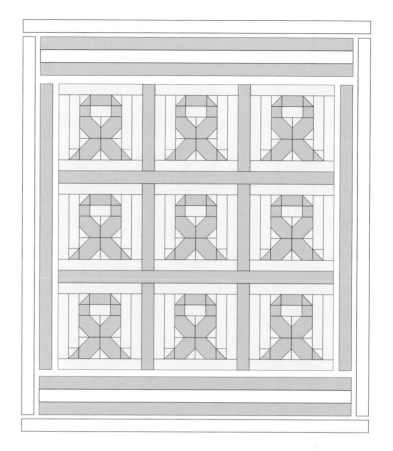

quilt from side to side in several places, again staying at least 6" to 8" in from the edges. Refer to Borders (pg. 111) for measuring and cutting instructions, if necessary. The quilt should measure approximately 44½". **Make 4 pink strips** and **2 white strips** that size or to your measurement.

Sew a pink strip to either side of a white strip. **Make 2**. Sew one to the top of the quilt and one to the bottom.

6 outer border

Cut (6) 2½" strips across the width of the fabric. Sew the strips together end-to-end to make one long strip. Trim the borders from this strip.

Refer to Borders (pg. 111) in the Construction Basics to measure and cut the outer borders. The strips are approximately 52½" for the sides and approximately 48½" for the top and bottom.

7 quilt and bind

Layer the quilt with batting and backing and quilt. After the quilting is complete, square up the quilt and trim away all excess batting and backing. Add binding to complete the quilt. See Construction Basics (pg. 111) for binding instructions.

tea
cakes

story contribution by Michelle Heber

When someone we love is hurting, making a quilt can be a healing gift for them as well as for ourselves. Michelle found that out when her friend faced a terminal illness.

I was just twenty-three years old when my dearest friend was diagnosed with cancer. The prognosis was not good; he was not going to live long.

The holidays were drawing near, and I was determined to find the perfect gift for what would most likely be my friend's last Christmas on earth. I wanted it to be something meaningful, something that could be enjoyed and used on a daily basis, no matter how unwell he felt. My friend was notoriously hard to shop for. As a young bachelor, he already had the all basics, and if there was ever anything he wanted, he didn't hesitate to buy it for himself.

I thought about getting him a dog for companionship, but quickly nixed the idea when I thought of the responsibilities of ownership. I thought about a trip filled with fun and memories, but as a struggling college student, I didn't have the funds for such a lavish gift.

In the end, I decided to make a quilt—my very first quilt. A quilt would give him warmth and comfort and remind him I cared even when I could not be by his side.

For the tutorial and everything you need to make this quilt visit:
www.msqc.co/blockholiday17

81

I decided on a simple design that I found in a book at my local library, a giant pinwheel placed in the center of a white block with a double border. As a high school home economics student, I had made a few items with my mother's hand-me-down sewing machine, but I was by no means a great sewist, and I had never attempted a quilt. But I just felt that I needed to do this—not just for my friend, but for myself. It gave me a way to start healing the sadness in my heart and to offer comfort to my dear friend.

I finished the quilt just in time for Christmas. It turned out just beautiful, even better than I expected. I wrapped it in a huge box topped with the prettiest bow I could find. When my friend opened the package, his face lit up and the tears in his eyes let me know that this was truly a perfect moment in a not-so-perfect world.

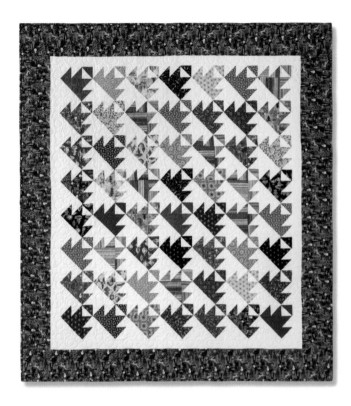

My friend cherished that quilt till his last days, and now it hangs on a quilt rack, a bit faded, very worn, and still holding all those special memories. It's much like our story; fibers woven together in the cloth of time gone by.

A quilt is such a precious gift. It represents so much time and care. When you wrap up in a quilt that has been made just for you, it is as if each stitch is there to remind you that you are loved! I hope you have many opportunities to experience the magic of giving and receiving such a precious handmade gift.

materials

QUILT SIZE
63¼" x 70"

BLOCK SIZE
6¾" finished

SUPPLY LIST
1 package of 10" print squares
1 package of 10" background
   squares

INNER BORDER
½ yard

OUTER BORDER
1½ yards

BINDING
¾ yard

BACKING
4 yards - horizontal seam(s)

OTHER SUPPLIES
1 package Cake Mix Recipe 2
paper by Miss Rosie's Quilt Co.
for Moda Fabrics

SAMPLE QUILT
Berry Merry by BasicGrey for
Moda Fabrics

1 layer and sew

Select 28 squares from each package of 10" squares. Set aside the remaining squares for another project or make your quilt larger.

Layer a print square with a background square with right sides facing and the lightest square on top. Pin a printed sheet from the package on top of the squares. Notice the star in the lower right corner that says, "Start." Adjust the stitch length on the sewing machine to make about 12 stitches to the inch. Begin sewing on the dotted line at the starting point. Simply follow the directions of the arrow points and continue to sew. Each stitch line is marked in the order it's to be sewn.

After you have sewn on all the dotted stitch lines, cut on the solid lines.

Remove the paper from each piece. You will have (2) 4½" finished half-square triangles and (10) 2¼" finished half-square triangles. Open and press the seam allowances toward the darker fabric. One paper makes (2) 6¾" finished blocks.

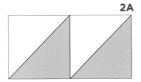

2A

2B

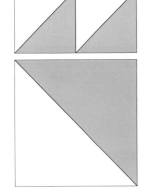

2C

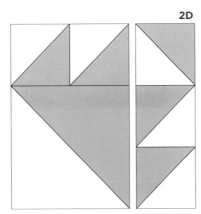

2D

2 block construction

Sew 2 small half-square triangles together as shown. **2A**

Sew 3 small half-square triangles together as shown. **2B**

Sew the row made up of 2 half-square triangles to 1 large half-square triangle. **2C**

Add the row of 3 half-square triangles to the right to complete 1 block. **Make 56. 2D**

3 arrange and sew

Arrange the blocks in **rows of 7**, then sew the rows together. **Make 8 rows.** Press the seam allowance of every other row in the opposite direction, odd rows toward the right and even rows toward the left. Sew the rows together to complete the center of the quilt.

4 inner border

Cut (6) 2½" strips across the width of the fabric. Sew the strips together end-to-end to make one long strip. Trim the borders from this strip.

Refer to Borders (pg. 111) in the Construction Basics to measure and cut the inner borders. The strips are approximately 54½" for the sides and approximately 51¾" for the top and bottom.

5 outer border

Cut (7) 6½" strips across the width of the fabric. Sew the strips together end-to-end to make one long strip. Trim the borders from this strip.

Refer to Borders (pg. 111) in the Construction Basics to measure and cut the outer borders. The strips are approximately 58½" for the sides and approximately 63¾" for the top and bottom.

6 quilt and bind

Layer the quilt with batting and backing and quilt. After the quilting is complete, square up the quilt and trim away all excess batting and backing. Add binding to complete the quilt. See Construction Basics (pg. 111) for binding instructions.

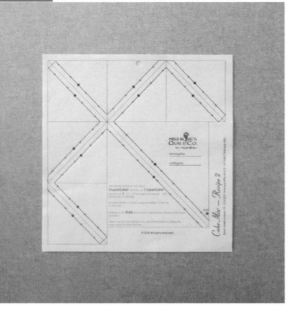

1 Layer a print square with a background square with right sides facing. Pin a printed sheet from Moda's Cake Mix Recipe 2 to the squares and sew on the dotted lines.

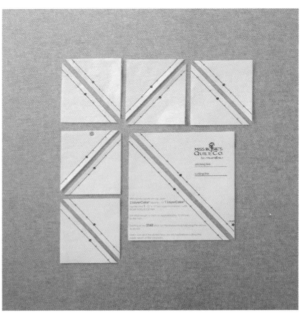

2 After sewing on the dotted lines, cut on the solid lines.

3 Sew 2 small half-square triangles together into a horizontal row.

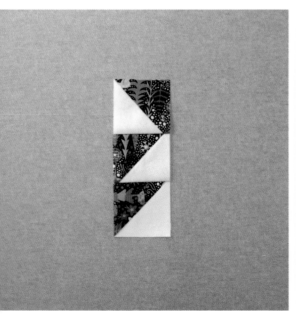

4 Sew 3 small half-square triangles into a vertical row.

5 Add a large half-square triangle to the horizontal row.

6 Add the vertical row of half-square triangles to the right to complete the block.

memory projects

Life is never predictable and we often experience loss right along with blessings. Sometimes the two can become so intertwined that it's impossible to have one without the other. When I heard this story, it inspired me to reach out to the Besse family and help them preserve memories of their beloved father who had recently passed away. All of these projects can be made with your loved one's clothing and will remind you of them for years to come. It can be difficult to know how to reach out in times of need and this is one way of showing love. -Jenny

Matt and I celebrated our ten-year anniversary back in November 2016. Together we have four incredible boys, aged two to nine. And in May we lost Matt to cancer. This story is not an easy one to tell, but as I share it with you, I feel gratitude for the time I was able to spend with this amazing man.

Rewind seven months to when we heard the three scariest words we could imagine, "You have cancer." Matt was diagnosed with stage four head and neck cancer. He had a canker sore on his tongue—at least that's what we had thought—that turned out to be a rare form of skin cancer. Matt had never smoked, drunk alcohol, or chewed tobacco in his life, so it was a complete shock to learn about his diagnosis. We were told that because there were no risk factors, it was a more aggressive type of cancer.

Last summer was hard, yet Matt still played, laughed, and wrestled with our boys, despite the tiring rounds of radiation he was going through. He was the happiest, strongest, and most positive guy I have ever known. He had incredible faith as he looked cancer straight in the face and fought with everything he had. In the midst of going through radiation, he still managed to be a fantastic husband and father.

Then, in December, Matt contracted pneumonia. At first he seemed to be getting better, but the infection came back. The x-ray revealed that he had a spot on his lung that kept getting bigger. Our fears were confirmed when he had a biopsy done and we found out the cancer had spread to his lungs. A few days later he was admitted to the hospital because he was having trouble breathing. We thought he would be home within in a few days, but God had a different plan for us.

Two weeks later we were told that his cancer was terminal. The doctor talked about quality of life over quantity and Matt came home to spend his last days with us. He died a week later, leaving behind four young boys. During this incredibly difficult time, there was, and continues to be, miracle after miracle! We believe that our Heavenly Father needed him home more than we needed him here on earth. In his short thirty-seven years of life and nine years of fatherhood, he set such an amazing example for our boys. He taught them about love, faith, strength, and hard work, among other things. He also taught them how to love their mother. Through his example he showed them that we can indeed do hard things! To say these last few months have been challenging is an understatement. Yet, I will treasure the time I got to spend with Matt and I am continually grateful to our wonderful friends and neighbors who have reached out to us with comforting words and kind actions.

-Holli Besse

memory projects

materials

TABLE RUNNER SIZE
14½" x 58½"

BLOCK SIZE
6½" x 14½" finished

SUPPLY LIST
9 assorted men's shirts
9 assorted men's ties

BACKING FABRIC
1¼ yards – horizontal seam(s)

BINDING
½ yard

BUTTON-DOWN SHIRT PILLOW
button-down shirt
batting or pillow form

MEMORY QUILT
QUILT SIZE
38" x 47½"

SUPPLIES
assorted men's shirts

BACKING
2½ yards – horizontal seam(s)

BINDING
½ yard

TABLE RUNNER

1 cut

From each shirt, cut (1) 7" x 15" rectangle. From each tie, cut (1) 12" – 13" length.

2 appliqué

Center a length of tie on the 7" x 15" shirt rectangle. Pin and appliqué in place using a buttonhole stitch or small zigzag. Make 9 blocks. **1A**

1A

Sew the blocks together, flipping the end of the tie 180° in each alternating block. Press the seam allowances in the same direction.

Layer the top with batting and backing and quilt. After the quilting is complete, square up the table runner and trim away all excess batting and backing. Add binding to complete the table runner. See Construction Basics (pg. 111) for binding instructions. **2A**

2A

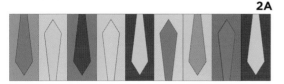

BUTTON-DOWN SHIRT PILLOW

1 cut & sew

Button the shirt and turn it wrong side out. Lay it out flat and mark a 16½" square onto the front of the shirt, centering the buttons and buttonholes.

Note: If using a pillow form, cut the square at least 1" larger than the form.

Using a rotary cutter, cut through both layers of the shirt. Sew all the way around the square. Trim the seam allowances at each corner to reduce bulk.

Unbutton a few buttons from the back and turn it right side out. Insert the pillow form or stuff with batting. Button the shirt back up to complete the pillow.

MEMORY QUILT

1 cut

From the back of assorted men's shirts, cut (2 - 3) 10" squares. The amount of squares you are able to cut will depend upon the size of the shirt. Cut a total of 20 squares.

2 arrange and sew

Arrange the squares into 5 rows with each row having 4 squares. Press the odd-numbered rows toward the right and the even-numbered rows toward the left. Sew the rows together to complete the quilt top. **3A**

3 quilt and bind

Layer the quilt with batting and backing and quilt. After the quilting is complete, square up the quilt and trim away all excess batting and backing. Add binding to complete the quilt. See Construction Basics (pg. 111) for binding instructions.

3A

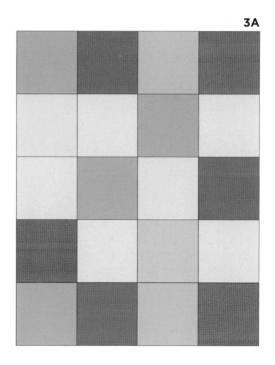

91

easy tube pillow case

materials

SUPPLY LIST
¾ yard focus fabric (pillowcase body)
¼ yard contrasting fabric (cuff)
2" x width of fabric (accent strip)

SAMPLE FABRIC
How the Grinch Stole Christmas by Robert Kaufman Fabrics

1 trim

Layer the three fabrics, one atop the other with the selvage edges on one side and the fold on the other. Using your rotary cutter and ruler, trim the selvages from all three pieces.

Fold the fabric for the accent strip in half lengthwise with the wrong sides together. Press. **1A**

2 layer

Lay the cuff out flat with the right side up. Place the pillowcase body atop the cuff with the right side up. Add the folded accent strip. Match up the raw edges of all three pieces and pin them together. **2A**

3 roll

Start at the bottom of the focus fabric and slowly begin rolling it up toward the cuff until it rests a few inches from the top edge. Bring the bottom edge of the cuff over

the rolled focus fabric and match the seams at the top and pin through all layers. This will make a tube with the cuff, focus fabric and accent piece inside. **3A**

4 sew

Sew through the 5 layers of fabric, using a ¼–⅜" seam allowance. This will enclose all the seams on the pillowcase except the side seam. Be sure you don't sew the end of the tube together! **4A**

Fold back the edge of the cuff and carefully pull out the body of the pillowcase. Turn the tube right side out and press the cuff flat.

Fold the fabric in half with right sides together being careful to match up the cuff and the accent strip. Pin to ensure that the pieces don't move as you sew.

Begin sewing at the bottom of the pillowcase (at the same end as the cuff) and sew to the top of the case. Then sew across the top of the case. This will be the shorter seam. After you have finished sewing the seams, clip the corners at an angle so the points will turn easily and lie flat. **4B**

If you choose, you can use a zig-zag stitch or use a serger to give the seams a finished look.

Turn the pillowcase right side out and press.

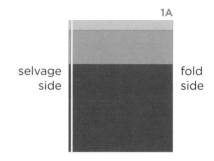

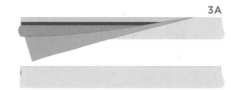

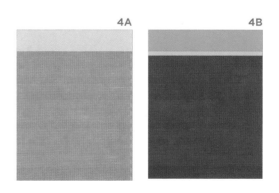

Quilt Tales
- a quilt along story -

Have you ever wondered what stories a quilt might tell? Do you find yourself daydreaming, longing for a little adventure? Let yourself be transported to a place outside of time and reality, and get lost in a magical world we've created just for you. Our favorite fairy tales have inspired us to create a unique quilting experience called "Quilt Tales." Each issue of BLOCK Magazine this year will contain a new chapter in a story to complement a quilt pattern. Stitch along with us and let your imagination run free!

The Forest Bride
By Nichole Spravzoff

BLOCK FOUR
TEA AND BISCUTS

"It's you!" Ingrid called out in amazement and clapped a hand to her mouth, almost dropping an apron full of buttons.

"Hello." Gustav smiled and gestured for her to hold out her hands. He tipped his handful of buttons into her palms and brushed off his knees as he stood.

"Why are you here?" She asked as she carefully poured the buttons into a small drawstring pouch, trying to tame the surprise in her voice.

He paused for a moment before he spoke. "I'm here to deliver a timber shipment," he said in his straightforward manner.

"Were you following me?" Ingrid didn't mean to accuse him, but she couldn't deny that he kept turning up places where she was and it unsettled her.

"For a bit, yes," he answered truthfully, with no hint of justification in his voice.

"Why?" Her eyebrows knit together and she looked at him intently, feeling more perplexed than ever.

"I want to talk to you," he said as he picked up her rucksack, hefted it onto his shoulder, and started walking, motioning her to follow.

She caught up with him in two quick strides and stepped in his path, blocking him from going any further. "What do you want to say to me?" Her hands were on her hips now and her stern demeanor caused him to take a step back.

He didn't answer her question directly, but sidestepped her

and pointed off to the right, "There's a tea shop around the corner. I think we should go there," he continued, steering her in that direction.

Ingrid hastened to keep up as Gustav strode across the square on his long legs. She was reluctant to join him, but curiosity got the better of her and she agreed to go inside the tea shop.

They stepped inside a cozy, wood-paneled room with a crackling fire and sat in the corner, obscured by a floral curtain in front of rippled, paned glass windows. There were few customers this late in the day. Most had gone home after their midday errands to prepare dinner. Gustav seemed immediately exhausted and he leaned one elbow on the table, propping up his chin.

"How did you even know I was here?" She asked, frowning.

"I spied you from the dock. Why did you try to hide?" He asked innocently.

A blush crept into Ingrid's cheeks and she tried her best to explain what had happened with Karl back at her cabin and why she was avoiding him.

"He came to see you?" Gustav looked puzzled. "That's odd."

"I agree. It's not as if we were … engaged." She almost whispered the last word of her sentence.

Gustav coughed and took a sip of tea. A full minute passed before the conversation continued with only the quiet clinking of spoons in between.

"So, why are we here?" Ingrid asked, feeling bolder away from the public eye. She rolled the napkin on her lap between her fingers, waiting for his reply.

He glanced toward the door. "I wanted to talk to you about something." He said in his simple, straightforward manner. If he had

something to say, he'd say it. And if he didn't, he was comfortable with silence.

"Go on." Her heart sped up as she considered what he might say.

His eyes seemed to focus on something beyond the room they were sitting in. "You know, I was there," he said, immediately serious.

"Where? At the feast?" She sounded confused.

"No, I was there. When Ivar …" He didn't need to say anything else.

Ingrid's eyes welled up at the memory of losing her childhood sweetheart. She had no idea Gustav had been there seven years ago at the accident that took Ivar's life. Gustav had been barely a man then, only fifteen years old and still in training to become a woodcutter. Ivar had just become a full-fledged woodcutter himself and was preparing to be married to Ingrid that spring when he lost his life in a logging accident. Ingrid had been told that the tree he'd felled hit a snag causing a large limb to come loose and strike him.

"Why are you telling me this?" She sniffed as tears started to drop from the corners of her eyes.

"You should have been with him. He was strong and kind. I admired him," he said, clearing his throat. "I'm sorry." He turned away to look at the fire.

"Thanks," she said, dabbing her eyes.

Gustav turned back toward her with a haunted look on his face. He hadn't planned on saying this much, but the words came out unconsciously and he knew he had to tell Ingrid the truth. "You shouldn't thank me," he practically choked out. "I was standing too close when the tree was felled. Ivar pushed me out of the

way ..." He couldn't finish the story. He stood to excuse himself and exhaled a ragged breath.

"Sit down," Ingrid whispered intently, looking about. She saw, through foggy eyes, that they were now alone. "Sit!" She insisted again, pulling on his sleeve. He sat.

"It's my fault." He couldn't meet her eyes.

"No. It's not," she said, disbelieving her own response.

"How can you say that?" He stared at her incredulously.

"Yes, you made a mistake," Ingrid's words flowed freely from her lips without a second thought, to her immense surprise, "but his death is not your fault. Ivar chose to save you. There's no way you could have known your mistake would cost him his life." She touched her cheeks in amazement; she'd had no idea those thoughts were in her mind. All of a sudden, she realized it was exactly the kind of thing her wise mother would have said. At that moment, Ingrid knew that the words she had said were true and she continued crying for an entirely different reason. Years of heartache were finally easing. Then she told him, "I forgive you," and meant it.

Gustav's face started to brighten as he looked over at Ingrid again and said, "That means a lot to me." She smiled in response and tentatively reached out to touch his arm. He gingerly placed his large, sun-browned hand over her pale fingers and said, "I've been carrying this guilt with me, believing I could have saved him," he said with relief creeping into his voice. His grip

tightened around her fingers and he met her eyes.

Ingrid's breath caught in her chest and her courage dwindled. Feigning a cough, she pulled her fingers out from under his to search for her handkerchief, rattling her teacup and spilling the remnants of her tea on the white tablecloth. "Look what I've done!" She wiped away her tears and started mopping at the tea stain, but it did no good. She stared at the delicate china cup, pretending to admire the hand painted design around the rim while trying to ignore the spreading stain. By the time a server came out to replenish their tea, they were sitting in near silence again, quietly munching on biscuits. Their words hung in the air, like the steam rising from the teapot.

When they left the tea shop, they were unsure how to part ways. What had taken place there seemed like it had been a dream and now they were fully awake as they stood blinking in the bright afternoon sun. Ingrid excused herself quickly, making some excuse about checking on her shipment of fabric. Gustav nodded to her and bowed slightly at the waist, as if he had escorted her to a soirée. He watched her walk away until she was no more than a speck against the blue sky.

Right then, as if on cue, Karl came up behind Gustav and clapped him on the back. "What have you been up to, little brother?" He jabbed him in the ribs and guffawed.

"Just stopped in for lunch. Are they done unloading the timber?" Gustav changed the subject back to the job at hand.

Karl nodded. "They just finished. Now, let's go get a couple pints to celebrate!" He thumped Gustav on the back once more and pointed in the direction of the nearest tavern. Gustav followed with the willingness of a whipped dog.

***

The following morning, Ingrid started her journey back to the village. So much had happened in two days that it seemed like she'd been in Skogsmark much longer. She was weary after a fitful night's sleep and almost immediately began dozing in the coach as it clacked over the cobblestone roads. When she awoke, the city was only a memory and she was surrounded by trees. It made her feel small and cozy, as if she were a beetle nestled between the fibers of a rug.

As the trip wore on, her exhaustion lingered. She watched the blue sky darken to gray and felt rain pound against the carriage. Spring storms were expected, but it soon became apparent that this one would be troublesome. Instead of a longing to be back home, Ingrid felt a foreboding feeling wash over her, as if something were wrong.

Harried, windblown, and soaked to the skin, Ingrid arrived back at her cabin to find a few large pines had toppled during the storm. One had fallen in such a way that it blocked her front door from opening more than a crack. Thankfully, it had missed the roof. She pushed her rucksack through the small, unlocked window in the kitchen, shimmied in with her skirts above her head, and fell to the floor in a clatter of pots and pans. Otto barked after her and she opened a lower window that had been latched and helped him inside. The wind whistled in the trees and the rain fell sideways through gusts of wind as she lit a fire in the hearth. "What do I do now?" She wondered aloud. It was at moments like these that she missed her father the most. He'd have taken one look at that tree, sized it up, and started chopping away. It would have been cleared by nightfall and stacked neatly next to the cabin for firewood. But as it lay right now, Ingrid acknowledged her inability to do anything about it, a feeling she rarely gave in to. She decided to sleep on it and set out to the village at daybreak in search of help and drifted off into a heavy, dreamless slumber.

to be continued...

block of the month

SUPPLY LIST

1 yard dark blue fabric

It's time to sew our center blocks together!

Sew the 4 variable star blocks together into a 4-patch formation as shown.

Sew 4 chevron blocks together into a row. **Make 4.** Sew a strip to both sides of the center.

Sew a pinwheel block to each end of the 2 remaining rows. Sew 1 row to the top of the center and 1 to the bottom.

Cut (6) 4½" strips across the width of the dark blue fabric. Sew the strips together end-to-end. Cut the borders surrounding the center medallion from this strip. Measure through the center of the quilt from top to bottom in several places. Cut 2 strips to your measurement, approximately 48½". Sew a strip to each side of the quilt. Measure through the center again, this time horizontally. Cut 2 strips to your measurement, approximately 56½". Sew one strip to the top of the quilt and one to the bottom.

This is not the finished quilt. Look for more to come in the next issue.

BOM 1 - Pattern found in Block Vol. 4 iss. 1

BOM 2 - Pattern found in Block Vol. 4 iss. 2

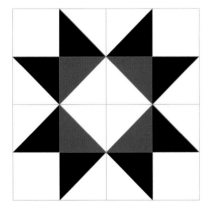

BOM 3 - Pattern found in Block Vol. 4 iss. 3

9-patch on point

materials

QUILT SIZE
75½" X 84"

BLOCK SIZE
8½" finished

QUILT TOP
1 roll of 2½" print strips
3½ yards background fabric

INNER BORDER
¾ yard

OUTER BORDER
1½ yards

BINDING
¾ yard

BACKING
5¼ yards - vertical seam(s)

SAMPLE QUILT
Holiday Flourish 10 by Peggy Toole
for Robert Kaufman

QUILTING PATTERN
Flower Swirls

ONLINE TUTORIALS
msqc.co/blockholiday17

baby block

materials

QUILT SIZE
42" x 42"

BLOCK SIZE
32" finished

QUILT TOP
4 assorted print 2½" x width of fabric
    strips or 1 roll of 2½" print strips
½ yard contrasting print
¾ yard background fabric

BORDER
¾ yard

BINDING
½ yard

BACKING
3 yards – vertical seam(s)

SAMPLE QUILT
Comfort and Joy by Dani Mogstad
for Riley Blake Designs

QUILTING PATTERN
Mitten Meander

ONLINE TUTORIALS
msqc.co/blockholiday17

candy
catcher
bag

materials

BAG SIZE
13½" x 15"

SUPPLIES
1 package 5" print squares
¾ yard contrasting fabric – includes
   lining and strap
25" x 40" scrap of batting

SAMPLE BAG
Eek Boo Shriek by Carina Gardner
for Riley Blake Designs

QUILTING PATTERN
Straight Lines

ONLINE TUTORIALS
msqc.co/blockholiday17

crossing paths

materials

QUILT SIZE
63" X 73"

BLOCK SIZE
10" finished

QUILT TOP
1 roll of 2½" print strips
1¼ yards light fabric – includes
    inner border

OUTER BORDER
1 yard

BINDING
¾ yard

BACKING
4 yards - horizontal seam(s)

SAMPLE QUILT
Forever Green by Holly Taylor
for Moda Fabrics

QUILTING PATTERN
Jingle Bell Roll

ONLINE TUTORIALS
msqc.co/blockholiday17

fancy fan table runner

materials

TABLE TOPPER SIZE
42" X 42"

BLOCK SIZE
9½" finished

TABLE TOPPER
1 package 5" print squares
¼ yard complimentary print fabric
1½ yards background fabric -
    includes border

BINDING
½ yard

BACKING
2¾ yards - vertical seam(s)

ADDITIONAL SUPPLIES
MSQC Dresden Plate Template

SAMPLE TABLE TOPPER
Very Merry by Kathy Engle for
Island Batik

QUILTING PATTERN
Free Swirls

ONLINE TUTORIALS
msqc.co/blockholiday17

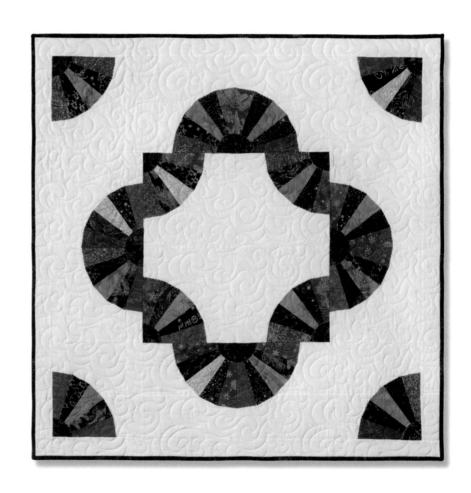

garden stars

materials

QUILT SIZE
68" X 68"

BLOCK SIZE
12" finished

QUILT TOP
1¾ yards red - includes outer border
2¼ yards background fabric -
   includes inner border
1¼ yards blue - includes corner
   stones and star points

OUTER BORDER
1¼ yards

BINDING
¾ yard

BACKING
4¼ yards – vertical seam(s)

SAMPLE QUILT
Studio Texture Delft by Timeless Treasures
Toscana Kiss Me by Deborah Edwards for Northcott

QUILTING PATTERN
Stars and Loops

ONLINE TUTORIALS
msqc.co/blockholiday17

home for christmas pillows

materials

PILLOW SIZE
16" finished

SUPPLIES
8 contrasting print 10" squares

BACKING
½ yard

OTHER
Pillow Forms to fit or your choice
of filler – Fiberfill, etc.

SAMPLE PILLOWS
Woodland Winter by Michael Miller
Fabrics

ONLINE TUTORIALS
msqc.co/blockholiday17

linked up

materials

QUILT SIZE
71" X 80½"

BLOCK SIZE
8½" finished

QUILT TOP
(1) package 5" print squares
3¼ yards background fabric –
    includes inner border
1 yard solid – sashing

BORDER
1¼ yards

BINDING
¾ yard

BACKING
5 yards - vertical seam(s)

SAMPLE QUILT
A Moose for Christmas by Cheryl
Haynes of Prairie Grove Peddler
for Benartex

QUILTING PATTERN
Champagne Bubbles

ONLINE TUTORIALS
msqc.co/blockholiday17

ribbons of hope

materials

QUILT SIZE
48" X 56"

BLOCK SIZE
12" finished

QUILT TOP
1½ yards pink – includes border
    strips
1½ yards background print

BORDER
¾ yard

BINDING
½ yard

BACKING
3¼ yards - horizontal seam(s)

SAMPLE QUILT
Studio Texture Pink by Timeless
Treasures

QUILTING PATTERN
Heart Large

ONLINE TUTORIALS
msqc.co/blockholiday17

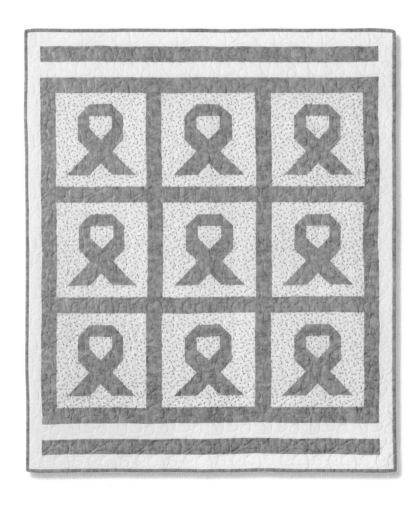

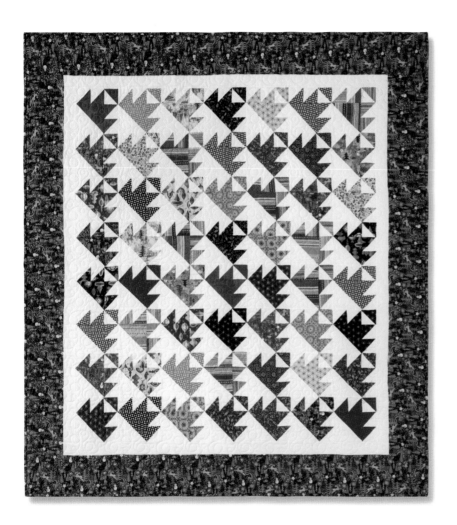

tea cakes

materials

QUILT SIZE
63¼" x 70"

BLOCK SIZE
6¾" finished

SUPPLY LIST
1 package of 10" print squares
1 package of 10" background
    squares

INNER BORDER
½ yard

OUTER BORDER
1½ yards

BINDING
¾ yard

BACKING
4 yards - horizontal seam(s)

OTHER SUPPLIES
1 package Cake Mix Recipe 2
paper by Miss Rosie's Quilt Co.
for Moda Fabrics

SAMPLE QUILT
Berry Merry by BasicGrey for
Moda Fabrics

QUILTING PATTERN
Loops and Swirls

ONLINE TUTORIALS
msqc.co/blockholiday17

construction basics

general quilting

- All seams are ¼" inch unless directions specify differently.
- Cutting instructions are given at the point when cutting is required.
- Precuts are not prewashed; therefore do not prewash other fabrics in the project.
- All strips are cut width of fabric.
- Remove all selvages.

press seams

- Use a steam iron on the cotton setting.
- Press the seam just as it was sewn right sides together. This "sets" the seam.
- With dark fabric on top, lift the dark fabric and press back.
- The seam allowance is pressed toward the dark side. Some patterns may direct otherwise for certain situations.
- Follow pressing arrows in the diagrams when indicated.
- Press toward borders. Pieced borders may demand otherwise.
- Press diagonal seams open on binding to reduce bulk.

borders

- Always measure the quilt top 3 times before cutting borders.
- Start measuring about 4" in from each side and through the center vertically.
- Take the average of those 3 measurements.
- Cut 2 border strips to that size. Piece strips together if needed.
- Attach one to either side of the quilt.

- Position the border fabric on top as you sew. The feed dogs can act like rufflers. Having the border on top will prevent waviness and keep the quilt straight.
- Repeat this process for the top and bottom borders, measuring the width 3 times.
- Include the newly attached side borders in your measurements.
- Press toward the borders.

binding

find a video tutorial at: www.msqc.co/006

- Use 2½" strips for binding.
- Sew strips end-to-end into one long strip with diagonal seams, aka the plus sign method (next). Press seams open.
- Fold in half lengthwise wrong sides together and press.
- The entire length should equal the outside dimension of the quilt plus 15" - 20."

plus sign method

- Lay one strip across the other as if to make a plus sign right sides together.
- Sew from top inside to bottom outside corners crossing the intersections of fabric as you sew. Trim excess to ¼" seam allowance.
- Press seam open.

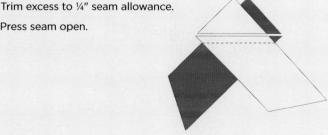

find a video tutorial at: www.msqc.co/001

attach binding

- Match raw edges of folded binding to the quilt top edge.
- Leave a 10" tail at the beginning.
- Use a ¼" seam allowance.
- Start in the middle of a long straight side.

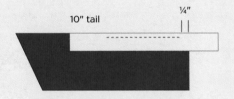

10" tail   ¼"

miter corners

- Stop sewing ¼" before the corner.
- Move the quilt out from under the presser foot.
- Clip the threads.
- Flip the binding up at a 90˚ angle to the edge just sewn.
- Fold the binding down along the next side to be sewn, aligning raw edges.
- The fold will lie along the edge just completed.
- Begin sewing on the fold.

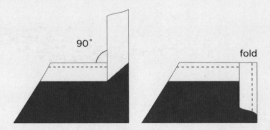

90˚   fold

close binding

MSQC recommends The Binding Tool from TQM Products to finish binding perfectly every time.

- Stop sewing when you have 12" left to reach the start.
- Where the binding tails come together, trim excess leaving only 2½" of overlap.
- It helps to pin or clip the quilt together at the two points where the binding starts and stops. This takes the pressure off of the binding tails while you work.
- Use the plus sign method to sew the two binding ends together, except this time when making the plus sign, match the edges. Using a pencil, mark your sewing line because you won't be able to see where the corners intersect. Sew across.

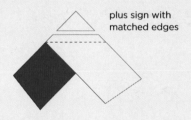

plus sign with matched edges

- Trim off excess; press seam open.
- Fold in half wrong sides together, and align all raw edges to the quilt top.
- Sew this last binding section to the quilt. Press.
- Turn the folded edge of the binding around to the back of the quilt and tack into place with an invisible stitch or machine stitch if you wish.